# Combating Money Laundering and Terrorist Financing

## A Model of Best Practice for the Financial Sector, the Professions and Other Designated Businesses

*Second Edition*

**COMMONWEALTH SECRETARIAT**

Designed and published by the Commonwealth Secretariat
Printed in Britain by Formara Ltd

Wherever possible, the Commonwealth Secretariat uses paper sourced from
sustainable forests or from sources that minimise a destructive impact on the environment.

Copies of this publication may be ordered direct from:
The Publications Manager
Communications and Public Affairs Division
Commonwealth Secretariat, Marlborough House
Pall Mall, London SW1Y 5HX, United Kingdom
Tel: +44 (0) 20 7747 6342
Fax: +44 (0) 20 7839 9081
E-mail: publications@commonwealth.int

ISBN 10: 0-85092-842-7
ISBN 13: 978-0-85092-842-6

www.thecommonwealth.org

# Contents

# Preface to the First Edition

Money laundering is a worldwide problem. It involves hundreds of billions of dollars that are laundered through international financial institutions. With increasing globalisation and liberalisation of financial systems, countries are becoming more vulnerable to the risks of money laundering and its contagious effects. The sheer scale of money laundering and the damage it causes warrant a strategic global approach. The work of the Financial Action Task Force (FATF) in formulating global policies to combat money laundering over the last 15 years has addressed the changing methods and techniques used by money launderers as they respond to evolving counter-measures. The FATF's original 40 Recommendations were drawn up in 1990 to combat the misuse of financial systems by persons seeking to launder dirty money, usually the proceeds of the narcotics trade and other criminal activities. In 1996, the Recommendations were revised for the first time to reflect evolving money laundering typologies. Following the terrorist attacks on the United States of 11 September 2001, the FATF issued a further nine Special Recommendations to combat terrorist financing, which sometimes involved the use of funds from legitimate sources for this illegitimate activity.

Following the increasingly sophisticated combination of techniques, such as the use of legal persons to disguise the true ownership and control of illegal proceeds and increased use of professionals to provide advice and assistance in laundering criminal proceeds, a comprehensive review of the Recommendations was undertaken and completed in June 2003. The process of revising the 40 Recommendations was extensive and open to FATF members, non-members, observers, financial institutions and other affected sectors and interested parties. The consultation process provided a wide range of inputs to the review. The Commonwealth Secretariat participated in the review process and the revised 40 Recommendations have been endorsed by the Commonwealth for implementation in all its member countries.

As part of its work in promoting good governance and combating corruption, the Commonwealth has over the years been in the forefront of international efforts to combat money laundering and terrorist financing, particularly through supporting its developing member countries in implementing comprehensive anti-money laundering (AML) and combating financing of terrorism (CFT) systems that comply with global standards. In 1996, the Secretariat developed generic Commonwealth Guidance Notes for the financial sector. The Guidance Notes were revised in 2000 and published as *A Model of Best Practice for Combating Money Laundering in the Financial Sector*.

It has been recognised that legislation alone is not enough to combat money laundering and terrorist financing; the financial sector and other associated businesses and professions must play a central and critical role. It is, therefore, essential for policy-makers to include the financial sector and other associated businesses and professions in the development of AML/CFT legislation and regulations.

This publication is a revision of the 2000 Commonwealth publication, *A Model of Best Practice for Combating Money Laundering*. It incorporates the new international standard arising from the revised 40 Recommendations and the nine Special Recommendations on Financing Terrorism.

I hope that this manual will be helpful for policy-makers, regulators, financial institutions and professionals, especially those working in the law and accounting and in designated businesses such as real estate agents and dealers in precious metals. At the macro level, it is intended as a tool for policy-makers in developing legislation and regulations; at the micro level, it seeks to provide guidance to individual financial institutions, businesses and professionals on combating money laundering and terrorist financing.

The manual is divided into three main parts: the first deals with global issues, strategies and standards; the second with national issues and, in particular, national strategy formulation; and the third with financial and professional sector procedures.

I am particularly grateful to Sue Thornhill and Michael Hyland of MHA Consulting, acknowledged international experts in the field, for their work in producing this publication.

**Winston Cox**
**Commonwealth Deputy Secretary-General**

# Preface to the Second Edition

The first edition of *Combating Money Laundering and Terrorist Financing*, published in 2005, has been warmly received by Commonwealth governments and professionals working on this problem, both in the Commonwealth and further afield. This second edition includes a number of minor corrections to the text throughout, and a new section on understanding how terrorism is financed. We hope that it will continue to be useful both to policy-makers developing legislation and regulations in this area, and to professionals working to ensure that they follow good practice.

**Indrajit Coomaraswamy**
Director
Economic Affairs Division
Commonwealth Secretariat

# PART I

# Global Issues, Strategies and Standards

# 1
# Background and Introduction

## 1.1 A Global Problem and Global Solutions

It is now over a decade since the first formal and concerted international action to combat money laundering was taken. At that time it was recognised that without effective international and regional co-ordination, there was little prospect of successful action to deprive criminals of the proceeds of their crimes. National economies also needed to be protected from the harmful effects of crime and its financial rewards. Global, regional and national initiatives and strategies all had their part to play in this concerted effort to combat serious crime.

Since the initial international initiatives were introduced, criminals have adapted, and money laundering methods and techniques have changed, in response to the counter-measures that have been introduced. As a consequence, the Financial Action Task Force, the principal international standard setting body, has fundamentally revised the 40 Recommendations that it drew up in 1990 and this has coincided with the revision by the Basle Committee of Banking Supervisors of its customer due diligence requirement for banks. In recognition of the way in which criminals have adapted to the international initiatives, the FATF Recommendations now extend beyond the financial sector to the legal and accountancy professions and to other designated business sectors.

In addition, since the events of 11 September 2001, the funding of terrorist activities has been seen as having many features in common with money laundering. In October 2001, the FATF issued its *Special Recommendations on Terrorist Financing*, containing eight additional special recommendations to supplement the FATF 40, and this was followed in April 2002 by a paper entitled *Guidance for Financial Institutions in Detecting Terrorist Financing*.

Most countries that had already established anti-money laundering measures have now added to their laws and regulations so that activities designed to provide funding of terrorist activities now come under the same level of potential scrutiny as money laundering activities.

As the Commonwealth Model of Best Practice inevitably draws heavily on the requirements of the FATF Recommendations and the Basle Due Diligence Principles for Banks, the Commonwealth Model has now been updated to reflect these changes to international standards.

## 1.2 Development of Commonwealth Anti-Money Laundering Strategies and Policies

The development of Commonwealth anti-money laundering strategies dates back to 1993 when the Commonwealth Model Law was drafted. However, at a meeting of senior finance officials in June 1995, it was recognised that legislation alone was not enough to combat money laundering. Criminals need to launder the proceeds of their crimes through the financial sector whose co-operation in combating money launder is essential.

Commonwealth Finance Ministers, at their meeting in Kingston, Jamaica in October 1995, endorsed the Report on Money Laundering Issues and actions produced by senior finance officials at their Colombo Meeting. Consequently, it was agreed to take action to follow up recommendations for the financial sector. Principal amongst these was the development of generic guidance notes setting out best practice in all areas covered by the legislation and offering examples of money laundering cases and potentially suspicious transactions.

*Commonwealth Guidance Notes for the Financial Sector* were first produced in 1996 and adopted at the Meeting of Commonwealth Finance Ministers held in October of that year.

It is recognised that for good practice guidance notes to be effective, they need to be reviewed on a regular basis to reflect changing circumstances and experience. Many changes in global anti-money laundering standards have taken place since 1996; while it is recognised that Commonwealth countries have progressed with the application of their legislation and financial sector guidance at different speeds, it is important that the *Commonwealth Guidance Notes* reflect current international standards. The Commonwealth Secretariat has therefore produced these revised *Guidance Notes* to reflect the changes that have taken place.

## 1.3 Purpose, Objectives and Status of the Model of Best Practice

Detailed best practice guidance for combating money laundering and terrorist financing can only be produced within the context of local national legislation and regulation and economic circumstance.

The approach to such legislation and regulation, which will reflect the local economic position, has a major impact upon the capability of the financial sector to play its required role. It is essential for the policy-maker to include the relevant parts of the private sector (together with all other parties involved) in the development of the legislation and regulation, and for the financial sector to make a full commitment to the success of the national anti-money laundering strategy.

This document therefore has two discrete but complementary purposes:

- Firstly, at a macro level, it is intended as a tool for policy-makers. It contains points of discussion for, and offers advice to, senior finance officials who, together with others, such as senior law officials, are tasked with drafting and monitoring a strategy which effectively involves the financial sector. In this respect, the document draws on the developing strategies and issues that have been considered by senior finance officials and Finance Ministers over the past five years.

- Secondly, it seeks to provide guidance to individual institutions and businesses on how they might effectively protect themselves from the damaging impact of handling criminal money and fulfil their obligations as regards anti-money laundering and terrorist legislation. Of necessity, this part of the document is of a generic nature, and each country must adapt it to reflect local legislation and regulation. However, the FATF Recommendations provide the world standard against which all countries will be measured and these have therefore been used as a base.

## 1.4  How to Use the Model of Best Practice

As indicated above, this document is intended to serve two purposes, and has been structured so that both purposes can be easily met.

- Part I (Chapters 1–5) sets out the general global issues and strategies to prevent money laundering. It also provides introductory definitions, and background information, which will be of interest and relevance to both national policy-makers and individual financial institutions.

- Part II (Chapters 6–9) assists the policy-makers who are preparing legislation, regulation and setting a national policy.

- Part III (Chapters 10–14) sets out the basis for financial sector policies and procedures and provides the options for adaptation by any individual country to reflect local legislation and strategies.

# 2

# Money Laundering: The Need for Action and the Benefits to be Obtained

## 2.1 What is Money Laundering?

Money laundering is the process by which criminals attempt to hide and disguise the true origin and ownership of the proceeds of their criminal activities, thereby avoiding prosecution, conviction and confiscation of the criminal funds. Failure to prevent laundering permits criminals to retain the funds or recycle them to fund further crimes.

## 2.2 Why Take Action?

In recent years, there has been increasing recognition of the need to attack money laundering in order to fight serious crime effectively. Former IMF Managing Director, Michael Camdessus, has estimated the amount of laundering at 2–5 per cent of the world's gross domestic product – almost US$600 billion, even at the lowest end of the scale. However, there are no estimates of how much of this is immediately spent by criminals and their organisations, and how much is laundered.

Of particular interest to the Commonwealth is the fact that, with the liberalisation of developing countries, laundered money can enter the financial system in the guise of assisting ailing economies and increasing inward investment. However, the unwitting acceptance of such 'dirty funds' can cause significant problems in the medium to long term as the funds frequently depart as swiftly as they arrived.

The ability to launder the proceeds of criminal activity, through the financial systems of the world, is vital to the success of criminal operations. Strengthening the prudential supervision and reputation of the financial system, the professions and other vulnerable business sectors through effective anti-money laundering measures is an essential prerequisite of achieving and maintaining the potential benefits of domestic and foreign financial liberalisation.

### 2.2.1 The Government View

From the point of view of national governments, there are four principal reasons for tackling money laundering:

- Failure to prevent money laundering permits criminals to benefit from their actions, thus making crime a more attractive proposition. It also allows criminal organisations to finance further criminal activity. These factors combine to increase the level of crime.

- The unchecked use of the financial system for this purpose has the potential to undermine individual financial institutions and ultimately the integrity of the entire financial sector. It could also have adverse macroeconomic effects and affect the exchange rate through large transfers of capital flows, and could lead to rent-seeking and distorted resource allocation.

- Unchecked laundering may engender contempt for the law, thereby undermining public confidence in the legal system and in the financial system, which in turn promotes economic crime such as fraud, exchange control violations and tax evasion.

- Money laundering facilitates corruption; ultimately, the accumulation of economic and financial power by unscrupulous politicians or by criminal organisations can undermine national economies and democratic systems.

### 2.2.2 The Financial Sector Interest

Both the financial sector as a whole and individual financial institutions have a keen interest in taking action. There are two principal reasons for this:

- The long-term success of the financial sector depends on attracting and retaining legitimate funds. These funds are attracted and retained because of the nature of the products and services, the quality and reliability of the service, and the reputation of the centre.

- Laundered money is invariably transient in nature. It damages reputations and frightens away the honest investor. The money launderer is a criminal and, if successful, will launch further attacks on the financial sector. It is therefore a matter of self-interest to protect the reputation of the financial sector by doing all that is possible to assist the authorities in detecting and prosecuting crimes.

### 2.2.3 The Interest of the Professions

While the long-term success of individual legal and accountancy firms is not so dependent on the reputation of the profession as a whole, greater public scrutiny is being given to professional integrity and any involvement by a professional firm with criminal money or terrorist financing will irreparably damage the reputation and long-term future of the firm concerned and will bring into question the integrity of the profession itself.

## 2.3 The Importance of Regional and National Initiatives: The Link to Economic Development and International Recognition

Crime is universal, but some countries export more of it than others. Countries lacking an effective criminal justice system pose a disproportionate threat to the wellbeing of more stable societies. They are a major source of cross-border flows of dirty money and one bad apple in a regional barrel can taint all of its geographical neighbours.

Some countries also appear more willing than others to import the proceeds of crime. Jurisdictions with inadequate financial supervision are often the ultimate destination of these flows. Money that begins life as the proceeds of a drug deal or an illegal arms trade is often laundered through a neighbouring country to avoid detection and confiscation in the country of origin.

An increasing amount of effort is being focused through the transnational organisations to reduce both national and regional vulnerabilities and to take action against crime and corruption. Increasingly, the level of international aid is being linked to the demonstration of political will to enact effective anti-money laundering strategies and to eradicate criminal finance and official corruption. Those countries that refuse to adopt international standards are finding that their economic development is hampered by a lack of international acceptance. Publicity is being given to the worst offending jurisdictions and financial institutions are being required to apply close scrutiny to transactions with these countries. Often, an entire region is affected and the need for both national and regional initiatives becomes vital.

The effects of this scrutiny is most apparent in the application of the FATF non-cooperative countries and territories strategy (see section 4.4) which recommends that countries such as the USA and the UK take measures to prohibit business with countries whose strategies to combat money laundering and terrorist financing and deemed to be wholly inadequate.

Experience suggest that the launderer favours institutions and services within poorly regulated, offshore havens, which offer guarantees of secrecy and anonymity. Such secrecy and anonymity is also available to the launderer through the informal channels of the parallel economy, (e.g. the 'kerb market' and the alternative remittance systems), which exist in a number of Commonwealth countries.

In recent years, significant international effort has been devoted to enhancing supervisory and regulatory standards and to developing international standards for combating abuse of the alternative remittance systems (see section 6.8). These measures to combat abuse must, of necessity, be implemented by both home and host states if they are to be effective.

## 2.4 The Money Laundering Process

There is no one method of laundering money. Methods can range from the purchase and resale of real estate, or a luxury item (e.g. a car or jewellery) to passing money through a complex international web of legitimate businesses and 'shell' companies. Initially, however, particularly in the case of drug trafficking and some other serious crimes, such as robbery, the proceeds usually take the form of cash. For instance, street level purchases of drugs are almost always made with cash, and this cash needs to enter the financial system by some means.

There money laundering process is often described as taking place in three stages:

- **Placement** is the physical disposal of cash proceeds derived from illegal activity;

- **Layering** is the process of separating illicit proceeds from their source by creating complex layers of financial transactions designed to disguise the audit trail and provide anonymity;

- **Integration** is the provision of apparent legitimacy to criminally derived wealth. If the layering process has succeeded, integration schemes place the laundered proceeds back into the economy in such a way that they re-enter the financial system and appear to be normal business funds.

The three basic steps may occur as separate and distinct phases. They may occur simultaneously or, more commonly, they may overlap. How the basic steps are carried out depends on the available laundering mechanisms, the requirements of the criminal organisations and the robustness of the regulatory and monitoring procedures of the financial sector.

Money laundering has traditionally been associated solely with banks and other similar financial institutions. Action to combat money laundering has therefore traditionally focused on the banks, reflecting the historical emphasis on the laundering of street cash derived from the sale of drugs. While it may be true that banking processes such as deposit taking, money transfer systems, lending, etc., do offer a vital laundering mechanism, criminals have responded to the counter-measures put in place by the banking sector and it must now be recognised that products and services offered by other types of financial and non-financial institutions are also attractive to the launderer.

Given the diverse channels through which money laundering proceeds are moved, an effective approach to combating money laundering must involve all aspects of the financial system. It must cover money that has already been 'placed' into the financial system and, of course, money derived from other forms of crime that has never been in the form of cash. The sophisticated launderer involves many unwitting accomplices:

- banks and securities houses;

- financial intermediaries;

- accountants and solicitors;

- surveyors and estate agents;

- company formation agents and management services companies;

- casinos and bookmakers;

- bullion and antique dealers;

- car dealers; and

- others who deal in high value commodities and luxury goods.

The basic techniques and mechanisms for money laundering continue to be well documented, primarily through the FATF typologies exercises (see section 4.1.5). A summary of this information is contained in Appendix A.

## 2.5 Basic Principles of Money Laundering Prevention

The following basic principles of money laundering prevention, contained in the FATF Recommendations, are common to all countries:

- Money laundering should be criminalised on the basis of the UN conventions and applied to all individuals and legal persons, determining as appropriate which serious crimes should be covered in addition to drugs (FATF Recommendations 1 and 2);

- Appropriate measures should be put in place to confiscate the proceeds of crime (FATF Recommendation 3);

- Banking secrecy laws must not conflict with or inhibit the effectiveness of the money laundering strategy (FATF Recommendation 4);

- Administrative and regulatory obligations to develop systems and controls guard against money laundering should be imposed on all financial institutions (FATF Recommendations 5–12, 15);

- Obligations should be placed on all financial institutions, that if they know or suspect, or have reasonable grounds to suspect, that funds derive from criminal activity, they should report those suspicions promptly to the competent authorities (FATF Recommendation 13 and 16);

- The obligations for developing anti-money laundering systems, controls and reporting procedures should be applied to designated non-financial businesses and professions, recognising, as appropriate, the concept of legal privilege (FATF Recommendations 16, 20 and 24–25);

- Financial and non-financial sector businesses, their directors and employees, should be protected against breach of confidentiality if they report their suspicions in good faith (FATF Recommendation 14);

- Appropriate, proportionate and dissuasive sanctions should be introduced for non-compliance with anti-money laundering or terrorist financing requirements (FATF

Recommendation 17);

- Countries should not approve the establishment or accept the continued operation of shell banks (FATF Recommendation 18);

- Countries should consider implementing feasible measures to detect or monitor the physical cross-border transportation of cash and bearer-negotiable instruments and to imposing a requirement on financial institutions and intermediaries to report all transactions above a certain amount (FATF Recommendation 19);

- Appropriate measures should be taken to ensure that financial institutions give special attention to business relationships and transactions whose anti-money laundering and anti-terrorist measures are inadequate (Recommendations 21–22);

- Countries should ensure that financial institutions, designated non-financial businesses and professions are subject to adequate regulation and supervision and that criminals are prevented from owning and controlling financial institutions (Recommendations 23–25);

- Appropriate law enforcement mechanisms should be put in place to process, investigate and prosecute suspected reports of money laundering and a Financial Intelligence Unit (FIU) should be established as the national receiving centre for information on money laundering and terrorist financing (Recommendations 26–32);

- Countries should ensure that the transparency of legal persons and structures can be accessed on a timely basis (Recommendations 33 and 34);

- Countries should rapidly, constructively and effectively provide the widest possible range of mutual legal assistance in relation to money laundering and terrorist financing investigations, prosecutions and related proceedings, and provide the widest range of international co-operation to their foreign counterparts (Recommendations 36–40).

Success requires the commitment of all involved, both within and across jurisdictions, including legislators,regulators, enforcement agencies and financial institutions. An important feature of money laundering prevention is partnership between all concerned.

## 2.6 The Benefits of Reduced Vulnerability

### 2.6.1 Environmental Protection

The impact of serious crime and corruption both within the developed and developing regions of the world is significant. Taking the profit out of crime can have a significant impact both socially and economically. Criminal money in large amounts undermines the social, economic and political fabric of society and consequently affects the day to day life and environment of every citizen. A relatively crime-free society with a sound and effective criminal justice system provides a healthier and safer environment in which to live and work.

## 2.6.2 Economic and Financial Analysis

The economic benefits of a sound, well-regulated financial system cannot be disputed and the fact that bad money drives out good is a well-known and documented fact. Ultimately, countries that fail to take action to guard against financial systems being used by criminals are in danger of having serious economic sanctions imposed upon them.

The involvement of national governments and regional/local institutions will lead to ownership of the problems arising from the laundering of criminal money and demonstrates the political will to act. Locally developed solutions will strengthen public and private capacity to respond effectively to new criminal threats as they arise. Strengthening existing institutional capacity within countries and regions makes these institutions more effective, more efficient and reduces their reliance on external assistance and donor aid.

Anti-money laundering programmes will help to identify and reduce fraud, tax evasion, breaches of exchange controls and other economic crimes. Procedures to follow the criminal money trail and confiscate the proceeds of crime can result in the ability to detect and recover significant amounts of corruptly diverted or embezzled government funds. The recovered and increased revenues can then be used for the benefit of society rather than increasing the wealth and profits of the criminal.

# 3

# Understanding How Terrorism is Financed

## 3.1 What is Terrorism?

According to the definition contained in the International Convention for the Suppression of the Financing of Terrorism drawn up in December 1999, the primary objective of terrorism is 'to intimidate a population, or to compel a Government or an international organisation to do or abstain from doing any act'. This is in contrast to other types of criminal activity where financial gain is generally the ultimate objective. While there is a difference in goals, terrorist organisations still require financial support in order to achieve their aims, and a successful terrorist group, like any criminal organisation, is therefore one that is able to build and maintain an effective financial infrastructure.

Terrorists and their organisations need finance for a wide variety of purposes – recruitment, training, travel, materials and setting up safe havens. Tracking, intercepting and strangling the flow of funds are vital elements of the global effort against terrorism.

The intelligence that can be gained about terrorist networks through knowledge of their financial transactions and dealings is vital in protecting national and international security and upholding the integrity of national and international financial systems.

## 3.2 Characteristics of Terrorist Financing

Terrorists often control funds from a variety of sources around the world and employ increasingly sophisticated techniques to move these funds between jurisdictions. In doing so, they draw on the services of professionals such as bankers, accountants and lawyers, and take advantage of a range of financial services products.

Although the total funds required by terrorist networks may be large, the funding required to finance individual terrorist attacks may be small. The US authorities have made an approximate estimate of the total cost of the planning and execution of the 11 September attacks in the USA of $200,000. UK experience bears out the relatively low costs required for an effective terrorist attack. The 1993 'Bishopsgate bomb' in the City of London, which caused loss of life and over £1 billion worth of damage to property, is estimated to have cost only £3,000.

Detecting the transmission of such relatively small sums as they move through the financial system is challenging, especially before a terrorist attack takes place. Nevertheless, disrupting the transfer of financial support for terrorism makes it harder for terrorists to operate. Tracking the flow of funds also provides information on links, profiles and movements, which helps to build up an intelligence picture of the way in which terrorists and terrorist organisations operate.

## 3.3 Sources of Terrorist Financing

It is generally believed that terrorist financing comes from two primary sources. The first is the financial support provided by nation states or organisations with large enough infrastructures to collect and then make funds available to terrorists. This so-called 'state-sponsored terrorism' has declined in recent years. Alternatively, an individual with sufficient financial means may also provide substantial funding to terrorist groups. Investigations have also revealed that some NGOs have been involved in the funding of terrorist activity.

The second major source of terrorist funding is legitimate or illegitimate revenue-generating activity committed by terrorist organisations themselves. Criminality can provide a consistent revenue stream and terrorist organisations will choose activities that carry low risks and generate large returns. The following financing activities are typical.

### 3.3.1 Extortion and Kidnapping

This form of fundraising continues to be one of the most prolific and highly profitable. Monies are usually raised from within communities of which the terrorists are an integral part in return for 'protection', usually against the terrorists themselves. Over time, extortion comes to be regarded as a cost of doing business in communities where it is prevalent, and payments from individuals or businesses become essential to obtain the release of kidnapped family members, colleagues or employees.

### 3.3.2 Smuggling

Smuggling across borders has become one of the most profitable activities for terrorist organisations. Successful smuggling operations require co-ordination and established distribution networks through which smuggled goods can be sold for profit. The illegal smuggling profits are 'placed' into the banking system with the use of front companies or short-term shell companies that are dissolved after they have fulfilled their purpose. Alternatively, legitimate 'front' businesses may be used to pay in the smuggled funds as part of their normal turnover. In some cases businesses extorted by terrorist organisations are coerced into placing criminal proceeds.

### 3.3.3 Drug Trafficking

The proceeds of drug trafficking activity can be a highly profitable source of funds for terrorist groups and nation states that sponsor terrorism. Even if a terrorist group is not directly involved in the importation or distribution of drugs, they often profit from the activity by allowing drug suppliers and dealers to operate within the communities that they control, and through the imposition of levies.

### 3.3.4 Charities and Fundraising

Community solicitation and fundraising appeals are a very effective means of raising funds to support terrorism. Such fundraising is often carried out by organisations which appear to have 'charitable' or 'relief' status. Fundraising activity may be targeted at particular communities where individuals either donate money knowing that it will be used for terrorist purposes, but more often believe that they are making a donation to a good cause. The charitable organisations to which they make donations often do, in fact, engage in some charitable work, in addition to acting as effective fundraising mechanisms for terrorism.

In line with the FATF recommendations, all countries are now required to take steps to prevent the misuse of charities for illegal purposes. Not all charitable or goodwill institutions, however, are as yet well regulated or required to maintain bank accounts. Charities are not required to publish full accounts of the projects that their fundraising efforts have helped to finance.

### 3.3.5 Donations

It is common practice within certain ethnic communities for amounts calculated as a percentage of income to be donated automatically to charity. Obviously it would be wrong to assume that such donations are either made with the intention of being of benefit to terrorists or that they are used for this purpose. Nevertheless, it must be recognised that both community donations and donations from wealthy private individuals and nation states that support terrorism are an important source of funding for many terrorist organisations.

## 3.4 Laundering of Terrorist-related Funds

As with other criminal organisations, terrorist groups will often attempt to obscure or disguise links between themselves and their funding sources. The methods used to achieve this objective are generally the same as for other criminal organisations (see Appendix A).

There have also been indications that some forms of alternative remittance systems, particularly the *hawala* system, play a role in the movement and laundering of terrorist funds.

Business relationships with individuals or entities that support or commit acts of terror will expose a financial services business to significant reputational, operational and legal risks. The risk is even more serious if the terrorists involved are later shown to have exploited ineffective systems of internal control or a lack of effective due diligence. The risk of funds intended to support terrorism entering the financial system can be reduced if financial services businesses apply satisfactory anti-money laundering strategies, particularly in respect of 'know your customer' procedures.

## 3.5  Recognising Terrorist Financing

It is important that, as with suspicions of money laundering, there should be a statutory requirement for all financial services businesses to report cases where they have knowledge, suspicion or reasonable grounds to know or suspect that funds are related to terrorist organisations or terrorist funding.

However, because of the inherent difficulty in formulating a suspicion before an act of terrorism has occurred, particularly when funding has derived from a legitimate source, it is acknowledged that financial services businesses may be unable to detect terrorist funding as such. The only time that terrorist financing might be clearly identified is when a client is recognised as being on a published list of terrorist suspects or organisations. Most financial disclosures are in fact made on the basis of suspicion of criminality and may not appear to be directly related to the financing of terrorist activity. The number of suspicion reports based on suspected criminal activity that have resulted in the provision of valuable information about terrorist groups highlights evidence of the important links between crime and terrorism.

## 3.6  Sanctions and Sources of Information

International action against terrorist financing has focused on the following:

- Sanctions to cut off money flows to individual terrorists and terrorist organisations;

- Standards to stop the financing of terrorism;

- Technical assistance to help countries develop the measures and infrastructure necessary to root out the financing of terrorism.

The Terrorism (United Measures) Order 2001 contains, *inter alia*, strict liability offences of making any funds or financial services available to, or for the benefit of, terrorists.

In November 2001, the IMF issued a communiqué calling on all member countries to ratify and implement fully the UN instruments to counter terrorism. UN Security Council Resolutions 1267 (1999) and 1373 (2001) requested each member within its jurisdiction to:

> freeze the assets of terrorists and their associates, close their access to the international financial system and consistent with its laws, make public the list of terrorists whose assets are subject to freezing.

In October 2003, FATF (see section 4.1.5) published a paper as a supplement to its eight special recommendations setting out international best practices for the freezing of terrorist assets which can be accessed on the FATF website (www.fatf-gafi.org). These best practices are based on the experiences of a number of jurisdictions, and are aimed at providing a benchmark for developing institutional, legal and procedural frameworks for an effective terrorist financing freezing regime.

The paper states that effective freezing regimes combat terrorism by:

(i) deterring non-designated parties who might otherwise by willing to finance terrorist activity;

(ii) exposing terrorist financing 'money trails' that may generate leads to previously unknown terrorist cells and financiers;

(iii) dismantling terrorist financing networks by encouraging designated persons to dissociate themselves from terrorist activity and renounce their affiliation to terrorist groups;

(iv) terminating terrorist cash flows by shutting down the pipelines used to move terrorist-related funds or other assets;

(v) forcing terrorists to use more costly and higher risk means of financing their activities, which makes them more susceptible to detection and disruption; and

(vi) fostering international co-operation and compliance with obligations under UN Security Council Resolutions 1267 (1999) and 1373 (2001).

The FATF best practice paper confirms that active participation and full support by the private sector is also essential to the success of any terrorist financing freezing regime. Consequently, it is advised that jurisdictions should work with the private sector to ensure its ongoing co-operation in developing and implementing an effective terrorist financing regime.

# 4

# Development of International Initiatives and Standards

## 4.1 Establishing the International Initiatives

International action to combat money laundering started in the late 1980s and the resulting developments have formed the basis for international standards and national initiatives. It is important that all Commonwealth countries adhere to international standards for money laundering prevention.

### 4.1.1 The Vienna Convention

A major impetus for co-ordinated international action to address three of the strategic tools came with the convening in Vienna in late 1988 of the UN Conference for the Adoption of a Convention Against Illicit Traffic in Narcotic Drugs and Psychotropic Substances. This Convention has now effectively been overtaken by the Palermo Convention of December 2002 (see 1.8.28) but in its time it provided a significant advance in the realms of international anti-money laundering matters.

The Vienna Convention, which came into force in November 1990, contained strict obligations. Countries which became parties to the Vienna Convention committed to:

- Criminalise drug trafficking and associated money laundering;

- Enact measures for the confiscation of the proceeds of drug trafficking;

- Enact measures to permit international assistance;

- Empower the courts to order that bank, financial or commercial records are made available to enforcement agencies, regardless of bank secrecy laws.

Article III of the Vienna Convention provided a comprehensive definition of money laundering, which has been the basis of virtually all subsequent legislation. It was also the basis of the money laundering offences in the draft *Model Law for the Prohibition of Money Laundering for Commonwealth Countries*.

In addition, the Vienna Convention provided for money laundering to be an internationally extraditable offence.

### 4.1.2 The Palermo Convention

Building on the successful Vienna Convention, the United Nations Convention Against Transnational Organised Crime was adopted by the General Assembly at its millennium meeting in November 2000 and was opened for signature at a high-level conference in Palermo, Italy, in December 2002. Of significance was the fact that it was the first legally binding UN instrument in the field of organised and serious crime.

Those signing are required to establish four distinct criminal offences in their own jurisdictions. These are:

- Participation in an organised criminal group;

- Money laundering;

- Corruption;

- Obstruction of justice.

Additionally spelled out are indications on how countries can improve co-operation on such matters as extradition, mutual legal assistance, transfer of proceedings and joint investigations. Moreover, those countries signing up commit to providing technical assistance to developing countries, to help them take their own measures to deal with organised crime.

### 4.1.3 The Council of Europe Convention

In September 1990, the Committee of Ministers of the Council of Europe adopted a new *Convention on Laundering, Search, Seizure and Confiscation of the Proceeds from Crime*. This Convention deals with all types of criminal offence, and so goes beyond the Vienna Convention. More specifically, the offence of money laundering was extended to include money laundering which is associated with all serious criminal offences. This was an important step in the fight against money laundering, as it recognised that the major criminal organisations do not specialise in one product alone, and added the impetus towards establishing an international 'all crimes' money laundering strategy.

### 4.1.4 The European Money Laundering Directives

The 1991 European Money Laundering Directive provided the basic standard for legis-lation and regulation amongst all European member states. A revised directive agreed in 2001 extended the scope beyond credit and financial institutions to corporate service providers, estate agents, casinos, lawyers and accountants. Any new country wishing to join the European Union must comply with the Directive as a condition of entry. The Directive also forms the base for many countries outside of Europe, and particularly the offshore financial centres.

### The Paris Convention

As an extension to the strategy contained within the second European Directive, a final Declaration Against Money Laundering, was issued following the Conference of European Parliaments on 8 February 2002. After a scene-setting preamble, analyses and proposals were presented under four separate headings:

- The transparency of capital movements;

- Sanctions against unco-operative countries and territories;

- Legal, police and administrative co-operation;

- Prudential rules.

Altogether a total of 30 proposals were recorded, setting out the high-level objectives for development of the anti-money laundering regime through the EU member states and the means whereby there could be greater co-operation and sharing of information than had previously been the norm.

### 4.1.5 The Financial Action Task Force

The Financial Action Task Force was founded at the 1989 OECD Economic Summit as a response by the heads of state of the G-7 nations to the growing problem of money laundering. Its mandate was 'to assess the results of co-operation already undertaken in order to prevent the utilisation of the banking system and financial institutions for the purpose of money laundering, and to consider additional preventive measures in this field, including the adaptation of the legal and regulatory systems, so as to enhance multi-lateral judicial assistance'. In 2001 the FATF extended its mandate to include measures to counter terrorist financing.

The FATF is a multi-disciplinary body, bringing together the policy-making power of legal financial and law enforcement experts and is regarded as the most influential and authoritative body in respect of money laundering policy and standards. The FATF has three main tasks:

- to monitor members' progress in implementing measures to counter money laundering and terrorist financing;

- to review money laundering trends, techniques and counter-measures, and their implications for the 40 Recommendations;

- to promote the adoption and implementation of the FATF Recommendations by non-member countries.

### The 40+8 Recommendations

In 1990, the FATF published 40 Recommendations aimed at governments and financial institutions. Together, these Recommendations formed a comprehensive regime against money laundering and have been accepted worldwide as one of the most comprehensive bases for tackling money laundering. These Recommendations were commended by the Commonwealth Heads of Government in 1993.

Originally, the FATF Recommendations were restricted to drug trafficking as addressed by the Vienna Convention, but in 1996 the FATF, having reviewed its Recommendations, extended them to cover all crimes. In October 2001, eight Special Recommendations to combat terrorist financing were published. The revised 40 Recommendations adopted by the FATF in June 2003 introduce a number of substantial changes to strengthen the measures to combat money laundering and terrorist financing. These include:

- The adoption of a stronger standard for money laundering predicate offences;

- The extension of the customer due diligence process for financial institutions, as well as enhanced customer identification measures for higher risk customers and transactions;

- The coverage of designated non-financial businesses and professions (casinos, real estate agents, dealers in precious metals/stones, accountants, lawyers, notaries and independent legal professionals, trust and company service providers);

- The inclusion of key institutional measures in anti-money laundering systems;

- The improvement of transparency of legal persons and arrangements.

The Recommendations and their interpretative notes form the basis for the guidance set out in Part II and Part III of this document. The complete text of the FATF Recommendations and interpretative notes can be accessed through the FATF website (*www.fatf-gafi.org*).

## Membership of the FATF

For many years, membership of the FATF was restricted to the principal 26 industrialised countries, of which five (Australia, Britain, Canada, New Zealand and Singapore) are Commonwealth members. However, in line with its new strategy for increasing the effectiveness of international anti-money laundering efforts, the FATF decided in 1999 to expand its membership to a limited number of strategically important countries who can play a major regional role. Argentina, Brazil and Mexico were admitted as members in 2000, followed by South Africa and Russia in 2003.

The minimum criteria for admission are as follows:

- To be fully committed at the political level
  (a) to implement the 1996 Recommendations within a reasonable timeframe (three years) and
  (b) to undergo annual self-assessment exercises and two rounds of mutual evaluations;
- To be a full and active member of the relevant FATF-style regional body where one exists, or be prepared to work with the FATF or even to take the lead in establishing such a body where none exists);

- To be a strategically important country;

- To have already made the laundering of the proceeds of drug trafficking and other serious crimes a criminal offence; and

- To have already made it mandatory for financial institutions to identify their customers and to report unusual or suspicious transactions.

Primarily, potential new members should belong to areas where FATF is not significantly represented in order to maintain a certain level of geographical balance.

### 4.1.6 United Nations Global Programmes

In support of concerted international action against illicit production, trafficking and abuse of drugs, a central tenet of the United Nations Drug Control Programme (UNDCP) is the development of global programmes against money laundering and of legal assistance.

The Global Programme against Money Laundering was set up to strengthen the ability of national law enforcement authorities and international bodies to fight money laundering more effectively. The strategy of the Global Programme is designed to achieve the following objectives:

- To increase knowledge and understanding of the money laundering problem and contribute to the development of policies by the international community of member states;

- To increase the legal and institutional capacity of states to fight money laundering;

- To increase the capacity of states to successfully undertake financial investigations into money laundering and matters relating to the proceeds of crime.

Composed of a multi-disciplinary team of legal, financial and law enforcement experts, the Global Programme provides advice and assistance to states in the development of anti-money laundering mechanisms; undertakes research on key issues; supports the establishment of specialised units; and provides training to law enforcement and justice officials for better implementation of money laundering laws.

## 4.2 Enhanced International Financial Regulation

Money laundering prevention is closely linked to sound financial supervision and regulation. Financial regulation around the world is governed by standards set by three main groups of regulators:

- The Basle Committee on Banking Supervision (the Basle Committee);

- The International Organisation of Securities Commissioners (IOSCO) for securities firms and markets;

- The International Association of Insurance Supervisors (IAIS) for insurance companies.

All three organisations have established principles of good regulatory practice to which most countries in the world are, at least nominally, signed up. These principles describe the appropriate structures for regulation, with requirements for independence from political interference and set out the features of a soundly regulated financial system.

In June 2003, the Basle Committee, IAIS and IOSO issued a joint Note providing a record of the initiatives taken by each sector to prevent money laundering and combat the financing of terrorism. The purpose of the note is to set out, in Part 1, an overview of the common AML/CFT standards that apply to all three sectors and, in Part 2, the variations for the three particular sectors. The Note explains that the AML/CML elements common to all three financial sectors are set out in the FATF 40 Recommendations.

### 4.2.1 The Basle Principles

Recognising the vulnerability of financial institutions, the Basle Committee on Banking Regulation and Supervisory Practices issued a Statement in December 1988 on 'Prevention of Criminal Use of the Banking System for the Purpose of Money Laundering'. This has subsequently formed the basis for much of the supervisory approach in this area.

Covering the basic issues of customer identification, compliance with legislation and law enforcement agencies, record keeping, systems and staff training, the Basle Principles have been generally endorsed by banking and other financial supervisors worldwide. Compliance with the Principles represents a major self-regulatory initiative within the financial sector.

Significantly, the Principles cover all criminal proceeds, not only those derived from drug trafficking, and can be implemented by the financial sector prior to the implementation of (or even in the ongoing absence of) a comprehensive legislative/regulatory programme to combat money laundering.

In October 2001, the Basle Committee issued a further paper covering customer due diligence for banks and addressing verification and 'know your customer' standards with a cross-border aspect. This reflected that earlier reviews of standards at national levels had found much variation and frequent instances where standards could not be judged as adequate. The role of national supervisors was recognised in respect of standard setting, and they are required to set their own standards with regard to what other nations are being expected to do to minimise variations at an international level.

While the Basle customer due-diligence principles were drawn up for the banking sector, the FATF drew heavily on both the principles and detail contained in them when undertaking the 2003 revision of the 40 Recommendations.

## 4.3 The International Monetary Fund

The International Monetary Fund (IMF) is an international organisation of 184 member countries that was established to:

- Promote international monetary co-operation, economic stability and exchange of information;

- Foster economic growth and high levels of employment; and

- Provide temporary financial assistance to countries to help ease balance of payments adjustments.

Since the IMF was established, its purposes have remained unchanged but its operations have developed to meet the changing needs of its member countries in an evolving world economy, which includes assisting countries in combating money laundering. In 2001 the IMF Executive Directors agreed a number of measures to intensify the work on combating money laundering, including more technical assistance for members, and agreed to extend its work to combating the financing of terrorism.

In recent years, there has been growing acceptance that setting international standards alone is insufficient; compliance with those standards must be maintained. Consequently, the World Bank and the IMF have taken on the responsibility for that task with particular emphasis on the core principles of banking supervision.

In November 2002 the FATF and the IMF formally approved a 12-month pilot project to include assessments on the adequacy of a country's measures to prevent money laundering and counter terrorist financing within the listed operational work of the Fund using the FATF Recommendations as the base standard. The detailed methodology for assessing compliance with AML/CFT standards that has been agreed between the FATF and IMF can be found on the IMF website (*www.imf.org*).

Closely linked to the IMF/World Bank assessments is the work of the Financial Stability Forum (FSF) which is looking in particular at the means of raising international standards within offshore centres, both in the area of financial regulation and anti-money laundering measures.

## 4.4 Action Against Non-co-operative Countries and Territories

Recent years have witnessed a sharp increase in the number of jurisdictions that offer financial services without appropriate supervision or regulation and are protected by strict banking secrecy legislation. In parallel, money laundering schemes have been characterised by increased sophistication and complexity where national boundaries are irrelevant. Global adoption of international standards has therefore become a vital requirement in the fight against serious international crime.

In order to ensure the stability of the international financial system and effective prevention of money laundering, it is recognised as essential that all financial centres in the world should have comprehensive control, regulation and supervision systems. Linked to this is the need for financial intermediaries or agents to be subject to strict obligations for the prevention, detection and prosecution of money laundering.

In preparation for international action to be taken against a country or territory whose legal, regulatory and financial systems do not meet international standards, the Financial Action Task Force has identified the detrimental rules and practices that obstruct international co-operation against money laundering.

The FATF's work on these so-called 'Non Co-operative Jurisdictions' covers all significant financial centres both inside and outside of the task force membership. In the event that any country so defined fails to take the necessary action, one of the financial sanctions to be taken could be the issue of an international OECD/FATF warning applying Recommendation 21 against the country concerned. FATF Recommendation 21 states that:

*Financial institutions should give special attention to business relations and transactions with persons, including companies and financial institutions from countries which do not, or insufficiently, apply these Recommendations.*

*Whenever these transactions have no apparent economic or visible lawful purpose, their background and purpose should, as far as possible, be examined, the findings examined in writing, and be available to help supervisors, auditors and law enforcement agencies.*

In June 2000 the first 15 non co-operative countries and territories (NCCT) were listed by the FATF and, subsequently, quarterly FATF meetings have led to many changes to the original list, both by new additions and by the deletion of those who have responded positively through new legislation and other measures. In 2002 it was announced that no more names would be added to the list, at least for a further 12 months, because the assessments that had been made by FATF would for the future constitute part of wider scope reviews to be undertaken by the IMF as part of the 12-month pilot project. However, countries that were previously on the list must still take the action necessary to earn their removal or face additional counter-measures by FATF members.

The FATF 2003 annual review of non-co-operative countries and territories and the various criteria against which jurisdictions have been judged can be accessed on the FATF website (*www.fatf-gafi.org*).

# 5

# Establishing International and Regional Co-operation

Money laundering is an international problem, often carried out by international crime syndicates, and effective measures to tackle it require international co-operation – no one country or agency can succeed alone. This co-operation is necessary at a number of levels, and between a number of different agencies.

The objective is to beat the criminals by applying the same basic standards internationally. Countries that delay in taking effective action risk opening the door to organised crime.

## 5.1 Co-operation between Governments

Co-operation between governments is vital to ensure that a legal and administrative framework exists for cross-border investigations into money laundering. At the most basic level, it is important that the legal and constitutional definitions of money laundering adopted by different governments are compatible, so that a crime committed in one jurisdiction will be recognised as such by others. The widespread adoption of the 40 FATF Recommendations, together with the 1988 United Nations Convention and the 1990 Council of Europe Convention, have greatly assisted in this process.

At the intergovernmental level, the processing of requests for international co-operation in money laundering cases is greatly eased by the negotiation of bilateral or multilateral treaties or agreements. In particular, Mutual Legal Assistance Treaties (MLATs), covering asset tracing, freezing and confiscation, the production of evidence and the questioning of witnesses, are extremely valuable tools in pursuing investigations across national boundaries.

However, international co-operation, or the deficiencies that exist, is an area that is frequently mentioned by countries as being a major obstacle to more effective anti-money laundering systems. Consequently, issues relating to international co-operation feature heavily in the FATF Recommendations.

### 5.1.1 Co-operation in Mutual Legal Assistance and Extradition

Because money laundering is international by nature, investigation into cases of money laundering are rarely confined to one country. To ensure that the investigation and money trail can be conducted cross-border, mutual legal assistance is required. During the review of the 40 Recommendations, the FATF identified two potential difficulties, or factors inhibiting more efficient and effective co-operation, namely:

(a) The requirement for a bilateral or multilateral treaty or agreement before assistance can be provided (as opposed to providing assistance on the basis or reciprocity); and

(b) The imposition of strict dual criminality requirements, both in relation to the criminal offence, but also with respect to the enforcement of foreign court orders to confiscate or seize the proceeds of crime. This effectively results in a court in the requesting country reviewing the decision of the court in the requesting country.

Consequently, the relevant FATF recommendations have been strengthened to overcome these difficulties.

Recommendations 36–39 now set out the additional basis for mutual legal assistance, stating in essence that:

- Different standards, definitions and predicate offences should not affect the ability or willingness of countries to provide each other with mutual legal assistance regardless of the absence of dual criminality.

- Countries should ratify the relevant conventions on money laundering.

- The powers to compel the production of records, search, seizure and obtaining of evidence should be available in response to requests for mutual legal assistance.

- Requests by foreign countries to identify, freeze, seize and confiscate the proceeds of crime should be dealt with expeditiously including arrangements for sharing confiscated assets.

- Mechanisms for determining the best venue for prosecution of defendants should be applied in cross border cases.

- Each country should enact measures to recognise money laundering as an extraditable offence.

### 5.1.2 Exchange of Information Relating to Suspicious Transactions

In recognition that obstacles were preventing information exchange and effective co-operation between national financial intelligence units, and that such obstacles can be removed through a foundation of mutual trust, the Egmont Group of Financial Intelligence Units was formed in 1997.

The objectives of the Egmont Group are:

- Development of Financial Intelligence Units in governments around the world;

- Stimulation of information exchange on the basis of reciprocity or mutual agreement;

- Access to the Egmont Secure Website for all FIUs;

- Continued development of training opportunities, regional/operational workshops and personal exchanges;

- Consideration of a formal structure to maintain continuity in the administration of the Egmont Group, as well as consideration of a regular frequency and location for plenary meetings;

- Articulation of more formal procedures by which decisions as to particular agencies' status vis a vis the FIU definition are to be taken;

- Designation of appropriate modalities for the exchange of information;

- Creation of Egmont Group sanctioned materials for use in presentations and communication to public audiences and the press about Egmont Group matters.

The development of FIUs is considered in Chapter 9.

There are now more than 80 national FIUs that are members of the Egmont Group and which are receiving suspicion reports and exchanging that information with their counterparts. Co-operation between administrative AML authorities was addressed in the 25 NCCT criteria, in particular:

- Not granting clear gateways;

- Making the exchange of information subject to unduly restrictive conditions;

- Prohibiting domestic authorities from assisting foreign counterparts;

- Obvious unwillingness to assist evidenced by undue delay.

Consequently, Recommendation 40 now includes enhanced requirements to assist the prompt and constructive exchange of information, in particular:

(a) *Competent authorities should not refuse a request for assistance on the sole ground that the request is also considered to involve fiscal matters.*

(b) *Countries should not invoke laws that require financial institutions to maintain secrecy or confidentiality as a ground for refusing to provide co-operation.*

(c) *Competent authorities should be able to conduct inquiries; and where possible, investigations; on behalf of foreign counterparts.*

The need for confidentiality in respect of exchanged information is recognised through the following statement in Recommendation 40:

*Countries should establish controls and safeguards to ensure that information exchanged by competent authorities is used only in an authorised manner, consistent with their obligations concerning privacy and data protection.*

## 5.2 Co-operation through Regional Bodies

Without doubt, the future of international money laundering prevention lies in the development and strengthening of regional groupings. A major development in February 1998 was FATF endorsement of a policy to strengthen the work of regional or other international bodies that already exist, i.e. the Caribbean Financial Action Task Force (CFATF), the Asia/Pacific Group on Money Laundering, the Council of Europe and the Offshore Group of Banking Supervisors (OGBS). The FATF report notes that the establishment of FATF-style regional bodies should rely, as far as possible, on existing structures, for example the Council of Europe or the Organisation of American States/Inter-American Drug Abuse Control Commission (OAS/CICAD), which are also able to assume responsibility for the fight against money laundering in their regions. Where a regional structure that can be adapted does not already exist, a new FATF-style body will need to be created. The development of FATF-style regional bodies will also be encouraged by the active involvement and support of one or more FATF members. Consequently, South Africa became the lead country within the Eastern and Southern African Anti Money Laundering Group (ESAAMLG) (see section 5.2.3) on gaining full membership of the FATF in 2003.

To encourage consistency in mutual evaluations, the FATF members recognise the value of inviting experts from FATF-style regional bodies to participate in FATF mutual evaluations and vice versa.

### 5.2.1 The Advantages of Developing Regional Approaches

The political, economic and social interests of countries are often affected by, and related to, the region in which the country is located. Actions by a neighbouring country perhaps have the greatest effect on its close neighbours, and in the areas of law enforcement and economic management this may be particularly true. There are few, if any, areas of the world where regional bodies which bring together the political and economic interests of members do not exist. These regional bodies provide the opportunity for essential interests to be pursued and for co-operative mechanisms to be developed. The common interest of members of the CFATF in the welfare of the region and the close relationship between that organisation and both the Caribbean Community (CARICOM) and OAS has undoubtedly led to its success within the region. Similar successes are beginning to emerge from the co-operation within ESAAMLG.

### 4.2.2 Developing Regional Standards

Perhaps the most compelling reason for countries to join with their neighbours to combat money laundering is that countries in regions or sub-regions often share particular problems and can benefit from the development of co-operative solutions. For example, it can be argued that the FATF Recommendations are most effective in countries which have structured and regulated financial systems and, most importantly, where cash is not the normal medium of exchange. The Recommendations work well, when implemented, in dealing with money laundering in the formal and non-cash sectors. They do not, however, address the issue of how to deal with, or detect, money laundering in economies which are cash economies and/or economies where reliance on a parallel banking system is the norm. Consequently, the Asia/Pacific Group has undertaken to develop specific recommendations in respect of this problem.

Specialist regional bodies are also in a far better position to judge the nature of their financial systems, the problems faced by them, the potential for laundering money through them and the best way to address the issue. This may mean that, while implementing the FATF 40 Recommendations, regional bodies will need to develop other specific regional recommendations to deal with the particular problems of their financial systems. Any specific measures should seek to ensure that money cannot be diverted from the formal sector and laundered through the informal sector.

Commonwealth countries may consider that there would be benefit in seeking to establish, either in conjunction with an existing regional body of which they are a member, or separately, a regional or sub-regional body committed to the implementation of anti-money laundering measures.

### 5.2.3 Current Regional Groupings

#### Caribbean Financial Action Task Force

Since its inception in 1990, membership of the Caribbean Financial Action Task Force has grown to 25 states of the Caribbean basin. The CFATF's additional 19 Aruba Recommendations are designed to supplement the FATF 40 Recommendations while specifically covering the particular regional issues relating to the Caribbean.

The CFATF monitors members' implementation of the anti-money laundering strategies set out in the Kingston Ministerial Declaration through the following activities:

- Self-assessment of the implementation of the Recommendations;

- An ongoing programme of mutual evaluation of members;

- Plenary meetings twice a year for technical representatives; and

- Annual ministerial meetings.

CFATF member governments have also made a firm commitment to submit to mutual evaluations of their compliance both with the Vienna Convention and with the CFATF and FATF Recommendations. The CFATF's first round of mutual evaluations will be completed by the end of the year 2000.

#### Asia/Pacific Group on Money Laundering

The Asia/Pacific Group on Money Laundering (APG) currently consists of 26 members in the Asia/Pacific region, comprising members from South Asia, South-east and East Asia and the South Pacific. Additionally, there are 11 jurisdictions with observer status (including the UK) and 15 observer organisations. The first annual meeting of the APG was held in Tokyo in 1998 and the 2002 meeting was in Brisbane, Australia. The 2002 meeting adopted eight Special Recommendations on Terrorist Financing and all APG members have undertaken to implement them. The APG continues its work to expand its typologies, in close consultation with the FATF and other regional bodies.

## Eastern and Southern African Anti Money Laundering Group

The ESAAMLG was launched in Tanzania in August 1999 and has grown since then to its present size of 14 member countries plus the UK and USA as observer jurisdictions, and the FATF, the World Bank and the Commonwealth Secretariat as observer organisations. The Group is committed to implementing the FATF Recommendations and Special Recommendations. A memorandum of understanding that was agreed at the inaugural meeting has been signed by 11 of the 14 member countries; Lesotho, Zambia and Zimbabwe have not yet signed up to their specific commitments to support the FATF Recommendations.

## South American Financial Action Task Force (GAFISUD)

The new FATF-style regional body, GAFISUD, was created in Cartagena, Colombia in December 2000. There are nine member countries. It has adopted both the FATF Recommendations and the Special Recommendations and has implemented a mutual evaluation programme.

## Inter-Governmental Action Group against Money Laundering (GIABA)

GIABA (Groupe Inter-gouvernemental d'Action contre le Blanchiment en Afrique) followed the December 1999 Summit of the Heads of State and Government of the Economic Community of West African States (ECOWAS) in Togo; the Group's statutes were approved at the ECOWAS meeting in Mali in December 2001. Provisional headquarters for GIABA are in Senegal but no agreement has been reached on funding for the Group.

## Council of Europe (Moneyval)

The Select Committee of Experts on the evaluation of anti-money laundering measures was established in September 1997 by the Committee of Ministers of the Council of Europe to conduct self and mutual assessment exercises of the anti-money laundering measures in place in the 25 Council of Europe countries which are not members of the FATF. The Select Committee is a sub-committee of the European Committee on Crime Problems of the Council of Europe (CDPC).

The membership of the Select Committee is comprised of the Council of Europe member states that are not members of the FATF.

The first round of mutual evaluations has been completed and a second round commenced.

## Offshore Group of Banking Supervisors

The conditions for membership of the Offshore Group of Banking Supervisors include a requirement that a clear political commitment be made to implement the FATF's 40 Recommendations. Members of the OGBS which are not members of the FATF or the CFATF are formally committed to the 40 Recommendations through individual Ministerial letters sent to the FATF President during 1997–98. Mutual evaluations of members who are not members of FATF or CFATF commenced in 1999. These have subsequently been replaced by the IMF assessments.

OGBS plays an active role both in FATF and the Basle Cross-Border Banking Sub-Committee and was active in developing the Basle Customer Due Diligence Principles.

### 5.2.4 *The Activities of Regional Anti-Money Laundering Groups*

The FATF, the CFATF and the Council of Europe Select Committee of Experts on the Evaluation of Anti-Money Laundering Measures (which have the widest coverage of the subject) have all developed core programmes of activity which include self-assessment of progress in implementing the 40 FATF Recommendations (and any other regionally agreed recommendations), mutual evaluation of national programmes and the monitoring of developments in the field of money laundering.

## Self-Evaluation Procedures

Commonwealth countries are familiar with self-evaluation of progress in combating money laundering. Finance ministers have mandated two rounds of self-evaluation and law ministers one round. These evaluations use exactly the same methods as those which are employed by the FATF and CFATF because they have proved successful and to save work for those Commonwealth countries which are members of one of the other bodies. The tabulated results of self-assessment surveys when distributed to members assist other countries to understand the laws of fellow member countries and, accordingly, provide a basic tool which can be used when seeking international co-operation.

## Mutual Evaluation Procedures

The 1991 Report of the FATF records a 'decision that underscores the great importance attached to the (evaluation) process' to initiate a process of mutual evaluation under which each member would be subject to being evaluated on progress measures three years after endorsing the FATF 40 Recommendations. Mutual evaluations are conducted by multi-disciplinary teams drawn from other member countries which look at the financial, legal and law enforcement aspects of a country's anti-money laundering efforts. In their early years, most evaluations concentrated on the state of a country's laws. More recent evaluations look closely at the effectiveness and implementation of those laws and at the operational aspects of combating money laundering.

The FATF was the first to adopt this process of peer evaluation followed by the CFATF. Most recently, the Council of Europe has put in place its own mutual evaluation process and the OGBS has agreed to a similar procedure among its members. Where a country is a member of more than one group which conducts mutual evaluations, the arrangements for evaluation are made between that country and the organisations of which it is a member, so that only one evaluation is conducted. For example, Cyprus, which is a member of both the Council of Europe and the OGBS, underwent an evaluation organised jointly by those bodies.

The mere knowledge that one's peers are to examine, at your invitation, your statute books, your banking and financial regulations and your law enforcement methods has the very real effect of ensuring that governments raise the priority of anti-money laundering efforts and make real efforts to meet standards. The prospect not only of having examiners visit your country but having their report discussed in a plenary meeting of all members of the group has an equally focusing effect.

One of the most important benefits of mutual evaluation is that it gives the examined country the opportunity to examine the effectiveness and implementation of national laws, regulations and operating procedures and provides a wider perspective on the national and international effects of anti-money laundering efforts.

## Monitoring Money Laundering Developments

One of the major activities of the FATF, the CFATF and the Asia/Pacific Group on Money Laundering has become known as 'typologies exercises'. Each of these bodies work actively to identify trends in money laundering methods and, perhaps more importantly, to consider emerging threats and effective counter-measures. The issues arising out of these typologies exercises are covered in Appendix A.

# PART II

# National Issues and Strategies

# 6

# Developing National Strategies

## 6.1 The Basis of Successful Anti-Money Laundering Strategies

Strategies to combat money laundering need to be wide ranging, involving the public and private sector working in partnership in legal, regulatory, financial and law enforcement fields. To ensure that any proposed anti-money laundering strategy is capable of achieving its aim, and of functioning effectively in a given political, social and economic environment, it is essential that laws, regulations and administrative actions are developed that take account of the context in which they must operate. This means that all interested parties should participate in the development and administration of anti-money laundering programmes from the outset.

Experience has shown that to achieve a successful anti-money laundering strategy within any jurisdiction, the following factors must be present:

- The political will to tackle serious crime and the associated laundering of the proceeds of those crimes;

- Effective legislation and obligations to criminalise money laundering;

- A comprehensive risk assessment and definition of the financial sector to ensure that all who are likely to be involved are covered;

- A supportive enforcement structure based on:
  (a) a central reporting point for suspicions of money laundering
  (b) trained financial investigators
  (c) guarantees of confidentiality
  (d) feedback from the law enforcement agencies;

- Management of the displacement factors and the informal sector; and

- Effective means of providing international co-operation.

### 6.1.1 The Formation of a National Co-ordination Committee

The formation of a dedicated National Anti-Money Laundering Co-ordination Committee (NCC) has proved to be an indispensable prerequisite to the success of the anti-money laundering strategy within a number of countries and has assisted in achieving the political will to succeed. The potential strategies chosen by each country will determine the people or the institutions who should be involved. However, the high level membership of the NCC should comprise individuals who can be expected to be impartial in their assessment of the national vulnerabilities, trends and objectives.

Recommendations for legislative, regulatory or policy enhancements must emanate from the NCC who must then determine the momentum for action.

It is suggested that the NCC might consist of the law ministry/attorney-general's chambers, the police and/or other special investigation bodies such as customs investigators, anti-corruption and serious fraud offices, the central bank/banking supervision and the finance ministry. These major governmental bodies will be in a position to assess various issues which will be relevant to the chosen strategy. In particular they will understand:

(a) The formal financial system, its general capacity and work methods;

(b) The criminal justice system including the capacity of the law enforcement sector and the constraints, if any, in the existing legal system;

(c) The capacity for international co-operation and mutual legal assistance;

(d) The civil law insofar as it relates to the relationship between financial institutions and professionals on the one hand and their customers on the other.

The NCC will need to take the preliminary decisions on the implementation of the FATF 40 Recommendations. Some of the Recommendations are mandatory and therefore require action to be taken. One such area is the requirement to report suspicious transactions (Recommendation 13). Other recommendations do not require mandatory action and the issue in respect of these is whether in all circumstances action is either necessary or possible. One of the subjects that falls into this category is the implementation of measures to detect or monitor cross-border currency movements (Recommendation 19(a).

## 6.2 Recognising Issues of US Extra-territoriality

Countries whose currencies are inter-related with the US dollar will need to have particular regard to the US anti-money laundering strategies. The USA will choose to apply its anti-money laundering legislation with extra-territorial effect if criminally derived funds are moved through the US dollar clearing system. US legislation provides the authority to take targeted, narrowly tailored and proportional action against those jurisdictions, foreign financial institutions or types of transactions that pose particular money laundering threats to the USA. Countries whose economies are heavily dependent on the US dollar should consider applying the US Treasury Office of Foreign Assets Control (OFAC) restrictions specifying designated nationals, funds or jurisdictions with which the USA does not permit business to be conducted.

### 6.2.1 The Extra-territorial Application of the US Patriot Act

The USA Patriot Act became effective on 26 October 2001, and although this is a US

Act many of its provisions are extra territorial in application and will therefore affect any institution which has dealings in the USA or with US-based banks. This extremely wide-ranging Act includes provisions on criminal laws, transporting hazardous materials, money laundering and counterfeiting, investigations and information sharing, federal grants, victims, immigration and US domestic security.

Specifically, the Patriot Act:

- Creates several new crimes, like bulk cash smuggling and attacking mass transportation systems;

- Expands prohibitions involving biological weapons and possession of biological agents and toxins;

- Lifts the statute of limitations on prosecuting some terrorism crimes;

- Increases penalties for some crimes;

- Requires background checks for licences to transport hazardous materials;

- Expands money laundering laws and places more procedural requirements on banks;

- Promotes information sharing and co-ordination of intelligence efforts;

- Provides federal grants for terrorism prevention, anti-terrorism training, preparation and response to terrorist acts, and criminal history information systems;

- Broadens the grounds for denying aliens admission to the USA based on their involvement with terrorism; and

- Alters some domestic security provisions, such as allowing the Attorney General to ask for the military's assistance during an emergency involving weapons of mass destruction and allowing the Department of Defence to contract with state or local governments for temporary security at military facilities.

### 6.2.2 Procedural Requirements – Money Laundering

The Act allows the Secretary to the Treasury to require domestic financial institutions and agencies to take certain measures when reasonable grounds exist for concluding that a foreign jurisdiction, financial institution outside the USA, class of international transactions or type of account is of primary money laundering concern. The measures include record keeping and reporting requirements, identifying certain information about owners or accounts and placing conditions on opening certain types of accounts. The Act establishes requirements on when and how the Secretary can impose these measures.

The Act also:

1. Requires US financial institutions to create enhanced procedures for certain types of accounts to detect money laundering;

2. Prohibits US banks from maintaining certain accounts for foreign shell banks (banks with no physical presence in any country);

3. Requires the Treasury Secretary to set minimum standards for financial institutions to identify customers opening accounts (including reasonable procedures to verify customer identity, maintain that information and consult lists of known or suspected terrorists or organisations provided by the government);

4. Requires regulations to encourage co-operation among financial institutions, regulators and law enforcement to deter money laundering (including sharing information about individuals, entities and organisations engaged in or reasonably suspected of engaging in terrorist acts or money laundering);

5. Requires the Treasury Secretary to adopt regulations requiring securities brokers and dealers to submit suspicious activity reports. (He may adopt similar regulations for futures commission merchants, commodity trading advisers and commodity pool operators.)

### 6.2.3 Criminal Provisions – Money Laundering

The Act creates the crime of bulk cash smuggling. A person commits this crime when, with intent to evade a currency reporting requirement, he knowingly conceals more than $10,000 in currency or monetary instruments on his person, in luggage or in a container and transports or attempts to transport it between the USA and somewhere outside the USA. This crime is punishable by up to five years in prison. Conspiracy to commit the crime is subject to the same punishment. Property involved in the offence is subject to forfeiture.

The Act also imposes criminal penalties on federal government employees and people acting on its behalf who, in connection with administering these money laundering provisions, corruptly (directly or indirectly) demand, seek, receive, accept or agree to accept anything of value for being influenced in performing an official act, committing or allowing fraud on the USA or being induced to violate his duty. The crime is punishable by a fine of up to three times the value of the thing received, up to 15 years in prison or both.

The Act increases civil and criminal penalties for money laundering. It adds a civil penalty or fine for certain violations by a financial institution or agency of between twice the amount of the transaction and $1,000,000.

The Act:

1. Includes foreign corruption offences, certain export control violations, certain customs and firearms offences, certain computer fraud offences, and felony Foreign Agent Registration Act offences as money laundering crimes;

2. Creates procedures for contesting confiscation of assets of suspected international terrorists;

3. Allows forfeiture of proceeds of foreign crimes found in the USA;

4. Allows forfeiture in currency reporting cases;

5. Allows certain Federal Reserve personnel to be considered law enforcement personnel and carry firearms to protect Federal Reserve employees and buildings.

6. Requires a study of currency reporting requirements.

The Act also makes various amendments relating to reporting suspicious activity, anti-money laundering programmes, penalties for violating certain provisions such as record-keeping requirements, maintenance of bank records and disclosures from consumer reporting agencies for counter-terrorism investigations.

### 6.2.4 Harbouring or Concealing Terrorists

The Act creates a new crime of harbouring or concealing terrorists. A person commits this crime if he harbours or conceals a person he knows or has reasonable grounds to believe has committed or is about to commit certain offences. These offences include destruction of aircraft or aircraft facilities; crimes involving biological and chemical weapons and nuclear materials; arson or bombing of government property; destruction of an energy facility; violence against maritime navigation; weapons of mass destruction crimes; acts of terrorism transcending national boundaries; sabotage of nuclear facilities and fuel; and aircraft piracy.

### 6.2.5 Material Support for Terrorism

The law prohibits giving material support or resources knowing and intending that it is being used to prepare for or carry out certain crimes. It also prohibits concealing or disguising the nature, location, source or ownership of that support or resources.

The Act amends this crime by expanding the definition of 'material support or resources' to include monetary instruments and expert advice and assistance. It also adds to the list of crimes that are the object of the support. The Act adds crimes involving chemical weapons, terrorist attacks and violence against mass transportation systems, sabotage of nuclear facilities or fuel, and damaging or destroying interstate pipeline facilities.

### 6.2.6 Forfeiture

The Act makes subject to the civil forfeiture laws all foreign or domestic assets:

1. of a person, entity, or organisation that plans or perpetrates a terrorist act against the USA or its citizens, residents, or property (this also applies to assets that afford someone influence over such an entity or organisation);

2. acquired or maintained by someone to support, plan, conduct, or conceal a terrorist act;

3. derived from, involved in, or for committing a terrorist act.

## 6.3 Developing Strategies for Offshore Financial Centres

### 6.3.1 The Potential Impact of Offshore Financial Centres

Many developing countries have looked to the development of offshore financial centres (OFCs) as a key to economic development. Consequently, the economies of many Commonwealth countries now depend, to some extent, on income generated by the offshore financial sector. Traditionally, the major offshore centres have been located in UK Crown Dependencies and Overseas Territories but other Commonwealth countries are also expanding their offshore banking services. The English-speaking Caribbean has a long history of offshore financial sectors with the first offshore operation established in the Bahamas in 1936. However, a paper published by the IMF in August 2002 found that apart from the British Virgin Islands and the Cayman Islands, whose offshore financial sectors accounted for 12.8 per cent and 3.9 per cent of GDP in 2000, and Antigua, which has reported that offshore banking accounts for 4 per cent of GDP, the majority of other islands' net revenues from the sector were well below 1 per cent of GDP. The report goes on to say that in a review of the Caribbean's experience, the authorities found 'solid evidence' of the benefits that have accrued to the economies of established centres but doubted whether newer centres would find it cost effective to operate in today's more stringent and initially more costly regulatory environment.

Of particular concern were the OFCs that began operating in the 1990s. The report stated that:

> *They must establish their operations in the glare of the international spotlight and, at least in the short term, they must absorb the cost of complying with international standards – costs that may readily equal the revenue gained from offshore financial activities.*

OFCs tend to attract business through offering a range of financial and professional services, combined with an attractive tax regime. Activity is primarily conducted on behalf of non-residents. Consequently, many become known as 'tax havens' and this is often believed to be synonymous with money laundering havens. This perception needs to be carefully managed.

Countries with significant or developing OFCs need to be specially aware of the particular attractiveness of the offshore financial services market to money launderers and national strategies need to take account of the enhanced risks. The particular characteristics of OFCs that might be adopted to attract foreign business through preferential tax treatment, exchange control incentives, minimal disclosure requirements, soft regulation and enforced secrecy are also of particular interest to criminals. For example, the misuse of international business companies and some offshore trusts set up in OFCs with strong secrecy laws are a cause of particular concern to the international community.

The UN Offshore Forum has identified minimum performance standards that must be achieved by all offshore centres. The performance standards have been set at a level within reach of all jurisdictions hosting OFCs, yet high enough to challenge mainstream jurisdictions as well. The performance standards incorporate core principles and standards promulgated by the FATF, the Basle Committee on Banking, Supervision and other international bodies.

The Report of the G-7 Financial Stability Forum released in May 2000 noted that offshore financial activities do not pose a threat to global financial stability provided they are well supervised and co-operate with other jurisdictions. However, the report concluded that OFCs that are unable or unwilling to adhere to internationally accepted standards for supervision, co-operation and information sharing create a potential systemic threat to global financial stability. International sanctions and reprisals can be expected against OFCs that remain in this category.

### 6.3.2 Criminal Threats to the Development of Offshore Markets

The expansion of global financial markets has not been without its problems. An issue concerning Commonwealth governments has been the increased volatility of capital flows as money has moved from market to market in search of short-term returns. A comparable threat comes from the increasing quantities of criminally derived and criminally controlled money flowing through the international system. These flows do not necessarily respond to normal economic stimuli, moving instead in response to changes in banking secrecy or financial regulation. Such movements result in unpredictability and hence the instability of the financial institutions through which they occur.

This instability should be of particular concern to those governments seeking to establish or develop their financial sectors. Criminal money may flow rapidly into new centres, providing an illusion of success and a short-term boost to national savings. They may equally flow away rapidly as conditions change, attracted by another centre, or merely moving to complicate detection.

Those governments that resist the temptation to soak up short-term flows from money laundering are likely to find themselves laying the foundations of a financial sector that can make a contribution to the economy over the longer term. By setting high standards of financial regulation, and by introducing effective money laundering counter-measures, they are likely to attract high quality financial institutions, which will not only provide a source of revenue directly, but which will contribute to wider economic development within the country.

While this point is relevant to all countries, it is particularly crucial to those seeking to develop as OFCs.

### 6.3.3 The Need for a Sound Regulatory Regime for the Offshore Financial Sector

Enhanced concerns of the international community about money laundering, tax evasion and terrorist financing have led to a number of concerted efforts to impose appropriate supervisory and regulatory standards on the offshore financial sector. In mid-2000 both the FSF and the FATF issued reports focussing on various offshore financial centres using various criteria to determine the degree of co-operation and/or the adequacy of legal and supervisory standards relative to international standards.

While domestic banks were generally covered by a strong regulatory regime conducted in accordance with the Basle principles and standards, this is not always mirrored by offshore banks which can be regulated to a variety of standards by ministries and other agencies. A strongly regulated financial sector without any distinction between onshore and offshore activities is an essential prerequisite for money laundering prevention. An adequate legal framework, clearly defined entry requirements, screening of owners and directors and an effective system of ongoing supervision are all necessary to protect the integrity of the financial system.

In response to the FATF's pressure, to OECD demands to end 'harmful tax competition' and to demands from the US following the 11 September attacks that all offshore banks should have a physical presence in the jurisdictions in which they are regulated, many offshore banks have been closed and the jurisdictions that host offshore banking sectors will need to continually revise their oversight standards. However, where high standards have been maintained, it has been possible for some OFCs to introduce progressively tighter regulatory requirements and anti-money laundering legislation without losing much legitimate business. Indeed, business that has been lost has soon been replaced by new higher quality business attracted by the higher standards that have been introduced.

## Relationships with Overseas Authorities

By their nature, regulators in OFCs are likely to have frequent contact with regulators in other jurisdictions, seeking legitimate information about the activities of financial institutions. At the same time they may well be subject to 'fishing expeditions' conducted by foreign revenue authorities, seeking information to help them develop a case against a suspected tax evader. It is important that the means exist to offer suitable co-operation in both cases, while not breaching confidentiality by responding inappropriately.

One of the most effective ways of achieving this is through the negotiation of Mutual Legal Assistance Treaties or, less formally, Memoranda of Understanding, with those jurisdictions that most frequently make requests for assistance. These agreements can specify the circumstances under which a request for assistance will be considered, the nature of assistance that might be provided and any restrictions that might be placed on the onward transmission of information.

### 6.3.4 Uses of Offshore Financial Centres

Offshore financial centres provide a number of legitimate and important services that can be broadly grouped into three categories:

1. **Private investments** in which investments are managed in order to minimise potential tax liabilities and maximise protection granted under statutory confidentiality provisions;

2. **Asset protection** in which the use of an international jurisdiction separate from the client's residence allows for the protection of income and assets from political, fiscal and legal risks; and

3. **Estate planning** in which the administration of assets is done in the most favourable legal and fiscal jurisdiction.[1]

The OECD Financial Stability Forum[2] has categorised the uses of OFCs as follows, some of which the Forum believes are more benign than others.

**Offshore Banking Licences:** A multinational corporation sets up an offshore bank to handle its foreign exchange operations or to facilitate financing of an international joint venture. An onshore bank establishes a wholly owned subsidiary in an OFC to provide offshore fund administration services (e.g. fully integrated global custody, fund accounting, fund administration and transfer agent services). The owner of a regulated onshore bank establishes a sister 'parallel' bank in an OFC. The attractions of the OFC may include no capital tax, no exchange controls, light supervision, less stringent reporting requirements and less stringent trading restrictions.

**Offshore Corporations or International Business Corporations (IBCs):** IBCs are limited liability vehicles registered in an OFC. They may be used to own and operate businesses, issue shares or bonds, or raise capital in other ways. IBCs may be set up with one director only. In some cases, residents of the OFC host country may act as nominee directors to conceal the identity of the true company directors. In some OFCs, bearer share certificates may be used. In other OFCs, registered share certificates are used but no public registry of shareholders is maintained. In may OFCs, the costs of setting up IBCs are minimal and they are generally exempt from all taxes. IBCs are a popular vehicle for managing investment funds.

**Insurance Companies:** A commercial corporation establishes a captive insurance company in an OFC to manage risk and minimise taxes. An onshore insurance company establishes a subsidiary in an OFC to reinsure certain underwritten by the parent and reduce overall reserve and capital requirements. An onshore reinsurance company incorporates a subsidiary in an OFC to reinsure catastrophic risks. The attractions of an OFC in these circumstances include a favourable income/withholding/capital tax regime and low or weakly enforced actuarial reserve requirements and capital standards.

**Special Purpose Vehicles (SPVs):** One of the most rapidly growing uses of OFCs is the use of special purpose vehicles to engage in financial activities in a more favourable tax environment. An onshore corporation establishes an IBC in an OFC to engage in a specific activity. The issuance of asset-backed securities is the most frequently cited activity of SPVs. The onshore corporation may assign a set of assets to the offshore SPV (e.g. a portfolio of mortgages, loans and credit card receivables). The SPV then offers a variety of securities to investors based on the underlying assets. The SPV, and hence the onshore parent, benefit from the favourable tax treatment in the OFC. Financial institutions also make use of SPVs to take advantage of less restrictive regulations on their activities. Banks, in particular, use them to raise Tier I capital in the lower tax environments of OFCs. SPVs are also set up by non-bank financial institutions to take advantage of more liberal netting rules than faced in home countries, reducing their capital requirements.

**Asset Management and Protection:** Wealthy individuals and enterprises in countries with weak economies and fragile banking systems may want to keep assets overseas to protect them against the collapse of their domestic currencies and domestic banks, and outside the each of existing or potential exchange controls. If these individuals also seek confidentiality, then an account in an OFC is often the vehicle of choice. In some cases, fear of wholesale seizures of legitimately acquired assets is also a motive for going to an OFC. In this case, confidentiality is very important. Also, many individuals facing unlimited liability in their home jurisdictions seek to restructure ownership of their assets through offshore trusts to protect those assets from onshore lawsuits. Some OFCs have legislation in place that protects those who transfer property to a personal trust from forced inheritance provisions in their home countries.

**Tax Planning:** Wealthy individuals make use of favourable tax environments in, and tax treaties with, OFCs, often involving offshore companies, trusts and foundations. There is also a range of schemes that, while legally defensible, rely on complexity and ambiguity, often involving types of trusts not available in the clients' country of residence. Multinational companies route activities through low tax OFCs to minimise their total tax bill through transfer pricing, i.e. goods may be made onshore but invoices are issued offshore by an IBC owned by the multinational, moving onshore profits to low tax regimes.

**Tax Evasion:** There are individuals and enterprises who rely on banking secrecy and opaque corporate structures to avoid declaring assets and income to the relevant tax authorities.

While all these services are designed to assist legitimate businesses, they will continue to be attractive to money launderers seeking to hide their illicitly gained assets. Those countries seeking to develop as OFCs must therefore be careful to deter criminal money, while still attracting legitimate international businesses. A sound reputation will be crucial for all OFCs as they move forward.

## 6.4 Establishing Co-operation and a 'Partnership Approach'

The success of any basic anti-money laundering strategy requires the commitment of all involved: the legislators, regulators, enforcement agencies, the financial sector and those within the professional and non-business sectors who will be covered by the AML strategies. Experience would suggest that an important feature of a successful strategy is partnership among all concerned.

### 6.4.1 The Role of the Financial Sector

The pivotal role that the financial sector can play is often also largely overlooked. A properly trained and motivated financial sector can make a substantial contribution to money laundering prevention, even in the absence of a workable criminal justice system. But equally, a financial sector that has not been consulted and trained, and which believes that the requirements are either an unnecessary breach of customer confidentiality, or are impracticable in their delivery, can frustrate even the best laws and investigatory capacity, while still working within the strict letter of the law.

In all jurisdictions throughout the world, the financial sector supervision and law enforcement elements of the anti-money laundering strategy must be regarded as complementary. The first is designed to prevent abuse; the second to deal with it when it occurs. This distinction is important but has not always been recognised by a number of countries preparing their prevention strategy.

### 6.4.2 The Role of Non-financial Professions and Businesses

Previously, AML strategies were confined to the financial sector and in some countries to banks and other credit institutions. It is now generally accepted that criminals have adapted to the counter-measures put in place by banks and for several years FATF typologies reports have referred to the increasing role played by professional service providers and non-financial businesses in money laundering schemes. Consequently, FATF Recommendation 24 now requires that selected non-financial businesses and professions should be subject to compliance with requirements to combat money laundering and terrorist financing taking a risk-based approach to their involvement. The money laundering risks associated with such businesses and professions have been recognised by a number of international bodies, including the European Parliament and the United Nations. The 1998 United Nations *Report on Financial Havens, Banking Secrecy and Money Laundering* states:

> *Money Launderers frequently use lawyers and accountants to help them hide funds. All too frequently unscrupulous lawyers provide advice on money laundering to their clients on the assumption that they will be protected by the rules of privilege that protects the confidentiality of the lawyer/client relationship.*

While professional privilege has been misused in the past, it is important that the concept of legal professional privilege in particular is honoured in any anti-money laundering strategy if the co-operation of the profession is to be obtained. Equally, the compliance regulations applied to other businesses must be applied on a risk sensitive basis if their co-operation is to be obtained. Applying financial sector requirements equally across the board will quickly lose support.

### 6.4.3 The Role of Law Enforcement

The role of law enforcement agencies within the prevention strategy is vital to the financial sector and the non-financial businesses and professions involved. If trust, respect and understanding between the two sectors are absent, the financial and professional sectors will withhold their co-operation in the fear that they are placing their staff at risk and breaching customer confidentiality unnecessarily. Suspicious transaction reports will not be made to a law enforcement agency that cannot be trusted to treat them confidentially, or which does not have the expertise to use the intelligence responsibly and wisely.

### 6.4.4 The Need for Reciprocity

Co-operation between the financial and professional sector and law enforcement needs to be reciprocal. Financial institutions and professional firms are acutely sensitive to any damage to their reputation and they will want the minimum of publicity about any money laundering investigations in which they become involved. Where they have effective anti-money laundering systems in place, the financial investigator's task of tracing criminal money will be facilitated and law enforcement agencies will tend to co-operate in keeping the operation out of the public eye. However, where a financial institution or a lawyer or accountant frustrates an investigation, there is less cause for the investigators to co-operate and the involvement of the institution in a money laundering operation is more likely to become public. This will lead to inevitable adverse consequences for the reputation of the institution or firm's reputation.

## 6.5 The Development of Policies

### 6.5.1 Legislative Policy

The following legal actions are generally required to ensure that the criminal justice system can provide a sound base for a national anti-money laundering strategy.

1. Laundering the proceeds of crime must be made a criminal offence in domestic legislation. Such legislation should make possible the identification, seizure and forfeiture of the proceeds of such crimes.

2. Full ratification and implementation of the UN Vienna and Palermo Conventions.

3. Enactment of measures that will permit or require financial institutions to provide to

competent national authorities information about the identity of their customers, account activity and other financial transactions.

4. A review of banking secrecy laws and making the necessary amendments to ensure that disclosure of financial institutions' records can be made available to competent authorities.

5. Assessing the need for increased multilateral co-operation and mutual legal assistance in money laundering investigations, prosecutions and extradition cases.

6. Adopting, where applicable, laws compatible with the Commonwealth Model Law for the Prevention of Money Laundering.

7. Implementing bilateral and multilateral agreements to allow for the equitable sharing between governments of property that has been forfeited as a result of co-operative efforts in the investigation and prosecution of money laundering cases.

8. If financial institutions suspect that funds stem from a criminal activity, they should be required to report promptly their suspicions to the competent authorities.

9. Financial institutions, their directors and employees should be protected by legal provisions from criminal or civil liability for breach of any customer confidentiality if they report their suspicions in good faith, even if they did not know precisely what the underlying criminal activity was, and regardless of whether illegal activity actually occurred.

10. Financial institutions, their directors and employees should not be permitted to warn their customers when information relating to them is being reported to the competent authorities (tipping-off).

The options for criminalising money laundering are set out in Chapter 7.

### 6.5.2 *Financial Sector Strategy*

Financial institutions will always be particularly vulnerable to money laundering and terrorist financing and they need to work with their regulatory and supervisory authorities in an effort to prevent the laundering of the proceeds of crime and to protect the reputation and integrity of the country's financial centre.

The vulnerability levels of any one financial centre to misuse by criminals are generally a direct result of the inter-relationship of the following factors:

(i) *The range of services offered by the financial sectors* – the greater the access to international markets, the higher the vulnerability. The provision of services such as off-the-shelf companies, anonymous accounts and bearer instruments only increases the vulnerability to criminal misuse.

(ii) *The size and maturity of the financial sector and the institutions* – the more immature the centre the less selective it can be as it seeks to maximise business opportunities within a highly competitive market, and therefore the greater its level of vulnerability. There is a similar vulnerability factor for the small immature institution even within a mature financial centre. The converse also applies in that the more mature the centre, or the larger the institution (especially branches/subsidiaries of international groups), the greater the selectivity of business that is required to protect their reputation.

(iii) *The effectiveness of financial sector supervision* – the nature and level of effective supervision will impact on vulnerability, e.g. the rigour of the licensing procedures, the frequency of ongoing compliance monitoring and the extent of variation between supervision of the onshore and the offshore sectors, will all affect the integrity and effectiveness of the financial sector.

(iv) *The existence of legislation criminalising money laundering* – opening the doorway to banking information and permitting asset seizure and confiscation will reduce the vulnerabilities.

(v) *The displacement factor* – while money laundering generally begins through the traditional banking sector, as preventative measures are taken in that area, so will the criminal extend his activities to the non-banking financial sector where regulation is often less stringent. Ensuring that supervision and regulation of all companies and businesses offering financial services is conducted to similar standards will provide a significant degree of protection.

### 6.5.3 Developing Strategies for the Non-financial Sector and Businesses

FATF Recommendation 24 states that:

*Designated non-financial business and professions should be subject to regulatory and supervisory measures as set out below.*

*a)    Casinos should be subject to a comprehensive regulatory and supervisory regime that ensures that they have effectively implemented the necessary anti-money laundering and terrorist-financing measures. At a minimum:*

- *casinos should be licensed;*

- *competent authorities should take the necessary legal or regulatory measures to prevent criminals or their associates from holding or being the beneficial owner of a significant or controlling interest, holding a management function in, or being an operator of a casino;*

- *competent authorities should ensure that casinos are effectively supervised for compliance with requirements to combat money laundering and terrorist financing.*

b)  Countries should ensure that the other categories of designated non-financial busi-
    nesses and professions are subject to effective systems for monitoring and ensuring their
    compliance with requirements to combat money laundering and terrorist financing.
    This should be performed on a risk-sensitive basis. This may be performed by a govern-
    ment authority or by an appropriate self-regulatory organisation, provided that such an
    organisation can ensure that its members comply with their obligations to combat
    money laundering and terrorist financing.

The Second European Anti-money Laundering Directive which was adopted in
December 2001 now applies anti-money laundering obligations to several additional
classes of businesses and professions which are believed to be at risk from abuse by money
launderers and terrorist organisations:

- Auditors, external accountants and tax advisers;

- Real estate agents;

- Casinos;

- Dealers in high value goods eg precious metals or works of art when there is a payment of €15,000 or more in cash;

- Notaries and other independent legal professionals, i.e. those who participate in planning certain types of transactions for their clients or act on behalf of their clients in
  any financial or real estate transactions.

Commonwealth countries will wish to consider the extent to which their anti-money
laundering and terrorist financing requirements include the specific non-financial businesses and professions that are designated in the FATF Recommendations and other
vulnerable business sectors (see Chapter 8).

### 6.5.4 Empowering the Financial Sector to Professions and other Businesses

Legislation on its own is not sufficient to construct an effective regime for preventing
money laundering. An appropriate institutional structure within which the law operates
is crucial and specific measures are needed to protect the financial sector from being used
to launder the proceeds of crime.

Many countries make the mistake of believing that they only need to concentrate
their efforts on enacting anti-money laundering legislation and on the role of the law
enforcement. Such a strategy may well serve to assist an investigation and prosecution
once a crime has been committed, but it will be of little use in preventing the proceeds
of criminal activity from entering the financial system, or preventing the laundering of
the proceeds of crime.

However, the commitment of the financial sector and its staff to the role that they
are required to play is an essential ingredient. Unless the financial sector itself 'buys into'

the obligations laid upon it and the underlying procedures, the strategy will have little effect. Hearts and minds must therefore be reached.

The role and contribution of the financial sector should be based upon compliance with the spirit of the Basle Principles and adherence to the FATF Financial Sector Recommendations. In essence, the financial and non-financial sectors contribution lies in:

- Knowing their customers;

- Keeping necessary records;

- Co-operating with the enforcement agencies through reporting of knowledge/ suspicion of money laundering;

- Providing other information promptly when legally required to do so.

However, money laundering legislation is not intended to turn financial institutions, professions and businesses and their employees into detectives. Staff should not be expected to go looking for signs of criminal activity, but neither should they be permitted to play a merely passive role. It is important that staff in the relevant professions and businesses are trained to recognise suspicions of money laundering and to report those suspicions at the earliest opportunity. While financial institutions and professional firms owe a duty of confidentiality to their customers, the maxim that 'there should be no confidence in iniquity' must apply. It is also a fact that no financial institution can afford to turn a 'Nelsonian blind eye' to possible criminal activities being carried on by its customers. Failing to ask the right questions merely to avoid receiving incriminating evidence should not provide any defence against a charge of assisting to launder the proceeds of crime.

The development of financial and non-financial sector obligations is considered in Chapter 8.

### 6.5.5 Enforcement Agency Policy

It is only through the full and effective enforcement of laws and regulations that money laundering can be prevented and punished, and the proceeds from illicit drug trafficking and other criminal activities be seized and forfeited. The effective enforcement of anti-money laundering legislation requires:

- The accurate and timely identification of persons, accounts and commercial transactions linked to criminal activity;

- The collection and analysis of such information in a timely fashion;

- Effective and timely investigations of the illegal laundering of the proceeds of crime in support of criminal prosecutions;

- The tracing and forfeiture of criminal assets.

In order to facilitate these aims, it is necessary to consider establishing or designating centres (financial intelligence units) within each country for the collection, analysis and sharing with competent authorities all relevant information related to money laundering. An effective enforcement policy also requires trained financial investigators to investigate the suspicions of money laundering ad to gather the evidence for a successful prosecution.

The options for financial intelligence and investigation units are set out in Chapter 9.

## 6.6 Identifying High-risk Business

### 6.6.1 Treatment of Countries with Inadequate Money Laundering Regimes

Given the international nature of both the global financial system and modern money laundering techniques, there is a danger that domestic action to tackle the problem will be undermined by criminal proceeds that have been introduced into the financial system from other countries. Once the money is in the financial system, it is harder to recognise its criminal origins and thus to take action against it. A comprehensive approach to tackling money laundering must therefore include measures to deal with these flows.

Each jurisdiction will need to take a view on those countries that the international agencies, e.g. IMF, G-7, FATF and OECD, specify as non co-operative jurisdictions and those with serious deficiencies in their money laundering strategies.

### 6.6.2 Risk Assessment in Financial and Professional Services and Other Business Sectors

Commonwealth countries will need to take a view on the level of risk attached to the type of financial and professional services offered within their relevant sector. Countries where cash is the normal medium of exchange will face an additional challenge and may need to consider imposing a mandatory cash transaction reporting requirement. As stated in section 6.3, the provision of offshore financial services, particularly those involving trusts and IBCs, present additional money laundering risks. Additional regulatory measures may be needed for the higher risk activities.

Financial institutions, the professions and other relevant businesses should be encouraged to take a risk-based approach to the products and services they offer when setting their anti-money laundering policies and procedures. This should involve having regard to the geographical location of their customer base and the extent of their business that is conducted in cash.

## 6.7 Identifying the Risks and Requirements for E-commerce and Internet Financial Services

E-commerce and the provision of internet financial services add a further risk dimension and open up additional mechanisms for fraud, money laundering and tax evasion. FATF Recommendation 8 states:

*Financial institutions should pay special attention to money laundering threats that may arise from new or developing technologies that might favour anonymity and take measures if needed to prevent their use in money laundering schemes. In particular financial institutions should have policies and procedures in place to address any specific risks associated with non-face to face business relationships or transactions.*

### 6.7.1 The Potential for E-money Laundering

The European Electronic Money Directive has defined electronic money as:

*Prepaid monetary value stored on an electronic device, which is issued by an entity and accepted as a means of payment by other parties. It is intended to act as an electronic surrogate for coins and bank notes and is generally used for transactions of a limited value.*

E-money is particularly useful for smaller value transactions where credit card costs become significant and their use is therefore prohibitive to merchants. E-money is also used to effect e-commerce person-to-person payments where the alternative may be a more time consuming off-line payment by cheque. Additionally, young persons and individuals without bank accounts may be provided with a convenient means of payment that does not involve the granting of credit. E-money may also provide an attractive means of payment that does not involve the granting of credit. E-money may also provide an alternative means of payment to consumers wishing to benefit from the budgeting aspects of pre-payment.

E-money products vary in design and technology. They may comprise accounts held centrally by the issuer where consumers and merchants open e-money accounts with the issuer and are then able to transact within the e-money system, or products may be based on smart cards. Smart card based products may hold the electronic money locally on the card, or in certain products may have both a local and central record of e-money balances.

E-money systems can be attractive to money launderers for two reasons:

### Untraceability

E-money systems provide anonymity allowing the parties to the transaction to deal with each other directly without the intervention of a regulated financial institution. Consequently, the required audit trail may be missing. Powerful encryption may be used to guarantee the anonymity of money transactions.

### Mobility

E-money systems may offer instantaneous transfer of funds over a network that in effect is not subject to any jurisdictional restrictions. Cash may be deposited into an unregulated financial institution. Placement may be easily delivered using a smart card or personal computer to buy foreign currency or goods.

## Managing the money laundering threat[3]

However, all e-money products give rise to opportunities for the detection of suspicious activity and for the means of limiting particular uses of the product. Account-based products are transparent to the issuer and may therefore be monitored for particular patterns and transactions. Non-account based products on the other hand can be restricted in their utility by the placement of controls on the smart card microchip. Such controls may, for example, require the card to be presented to the issuer at regular intervals, based on the satisfaction of certain conditions such as turnover limits or number of transactions conducted, failing which purses would cease to operate. Such purses can also be restricted in terms of the type of other purses with which they can transact (consumer, merchant, issuer, etc.). This allows for a flexible means of devising appropriate 'purse controls' so as to minimise the utility of purses for money laundering.

### 6.7.2 Internet Banking

FATF typologies exercises have identified the following concerns regarding on-line banking and money laundering:

(a) The reduction in face-to-face contact;

(b) The inability or increased difficulty in verifying the identity of the customer opening and accessing an account on-line;

(c) Increased difficulty in identifying the person controlling the account and determining what is normal account activity;

(d) A possible lack of investigative or regulatory jurisdiction.

The FATF has put forward the following suggestions to prevent internet banking services being used by money launderers:

(a) The need for financial institutions offering internet banking services to have a full and proper customer identification procedure, including identifying the person, their address, etc. This should include checking and verifying original or certified copies of appropriate identification documents by bank branches or other trusted third parties, and this should be checked by internal and external audit.

(b) Using 'know your customer' policies to obtain initial information on the client, their needs, the source of funds and likely client and transaction profile; and then to monitor or review account activity and have in place a system to red flag potentially suspicious transactions.

(c) Ensuring that e-money institutions are properly regulated (and that they are regarded as financial institutions for the purpose of anti-money laundering controls).

(d) Ensuring that record keeping for electronic transactions is complete and thorough, and sufficient details are kept to construct an audit trail.

To assist the ability to follow the links between criminal proceeds and the individual attempting to launder them, the following additional suggestions have been made:

(a) Require Internet Service Providers (ISPs) to maintain reliable subscriber registers with appropriate identification information;

(b) Require ISPs to establish log files with traffic data relating the Internet-protocol number to the subscriber and to the telephone number used in the connection;

(c) Require that this information be maintained for a reasonable period (six months to a year);

(d) Ensure that this information is made available internationally in a timely manner when criminal investigations are being conducted.

## 6.8 Managing the Displacement Factors: Parallel Economies, Underground Banking and Alternative Remittance Systems

In many countries it is recognised that there is a significant 'parallel economy' in which money circulates outside the conventional financial system. The global spread of ethnic groups from Asia and China has provided a worldwide network for the underground banking systems variously known as *hawala*, *hundi* or *chiti* banking. Through these systems, funds or value can be transferred from individual to individual, or from country to country or any combination of them. However, the service is traditionally provided without questions, and without paperwork or the inevitable audit trail that recognised banking procedures entail. Consequently, the nature of the system is such that the anonymity of its customers is assured and those tasked with monetary control and surveillance find it almost impossible to examine.

### 6.8.1 Criminal Use of Alternative Remittance Systems

While alternative remittance systems have a long tradition of legitimate and efficient uses, they are also purpose-made for criminal transactions. As the systems do not leave an audit trail, the criminal stands a great a chance of laundering his funds without detection, and consequently of retaining their use, as legitimate earnings. Evidence shows that criminals involved in illicit arms and gold smuggling, drug trafficking, terrorist related crimes, fraud, bribery and corruption are using the alternative remittance systems on an increasing scale.

In response to the widespread concern that criminal use of the underground systems will continue to increase as more countries enact legislation to trace and confiscate the proceeds of crime passing through the international regulated banking system, FATF Recommendation 23 concerning the licensing, regulation and supervision of financial institutions states that:

> ... at a minimum, businesses providing a service of money or value transfer, or of money or currency changing should be licensed or registered, and subject to effective systems for monitoring and ensuring compliance with national requirements to combat money laundering and terrorist financing.

In addition, FATF Special Recommendation VI: Alternative Remittance systems within the Special Recommendations on Terrorist Financing requires that:

> Each country should take measures to ensure that persons or legal entities, including agents, that provide a service for the transmission of money or value, including transmission through an informal money or value transfer system or network, should be licensed or registered and subject to all the FATF Recommendations that apply to banks and non-bank financial institutions. Each country should ensure that persons or legal entities that carry out this service illegally are subject to administrative, civil or criminal sanctions.

The Interpretative Note to Special Recommendation VI advises that its objective is to increase the transparency of payment flows by ensuring that jurisdictions impose consistent anti-money laundering and counter-terrorist financing measures on all forms of money/value transfer systems, particularly those traditionally operating outside the conventional financial sector and not previously subject to the FATF Recommendations.

In June 2003 FATF supplemented its recommendations on alternative remittance systems with an International Best Practice paper on the subject covering:

- Definition of money or value services
- Statement of problem
- Principles
- Areas of focus
  - licensing/registration
  - identification and awareness raising
  - anti-money laundering regulations
  - compliance monitoring
  - sanctions.

### 6.8.2 Identifying the Existence of Alternative Remittance/Money Value Transfer Systems

The FATF Best Practice paper advises that for the majority of jurisdictions, proactive identification of informal money value transfer services is an integral element of establishing and maintaining an effective registration/licensing regime. Suggested best practices to identify alternative remittance/money value transfer services include:

- Examining newspapers and other media to detect advertising and monitoring activities in neighbourhoods where such systems are likely to operate;

- Encouraging investigative agencies to pay particular attention to ledgers of business that may be associated with such systems and examining patterns of activity that may indicate such activity;

- Consulting with the operators of registered/licensed services for potential leads on those who are operating without registration or licence;

- Paying attention to the users of bulk currency and using couriers as a source of intelligence;

- Paying particular attention to suspicion reports from the regulated sector that might indicate a link to alternative remittance systems;

- Assisting banks and other financial institutions in developing an understanding of what activities/indications are suggestive of alternative remittance systems and informal money value transfer operations and giving banks that authority to cross-check particular accounts against a register of operators.

### 6.8.3 Implementing Counter-measures

In addition to the work of the FATF, studies undertaken on behalf of Commonwealth Ministers have identified a number of counter-measures that can be considered for preventing wider use of the underground banking and remittance systems for money laundering:

- Increased co-ordination of action within developing countries to conserve foreign exchange and prevent its leakage;

- Removing the incentives for use of the alternative remittance systems by law-abiding citizens and isolating the criminal use;

- Improving regulation and inspection to reduce smuggling and duty evasion;

- Ensuring that money laundering legislation and regulations embrace within their scope all financial activities, including money transmission and foreign exchange operations rather than defining the scope by type of institution;

- Ensuring that all businesses within the scope of the money laundering legislation are authorised, supervised, inspected and sanctioned for non-compliance;

- Introducing the concept of wilful blindness, i.e. should have known or suspected that the money could not have been legally earned or legally transferred;

- Introducing a compulsory transaction reporting requirement linked to a strict regime of monitoring and regulation with criminal penalties for non compliance.

### 6.8.4 Counter-measures Using the Interface with the Formal Banking System

The underground banking system is at its most vulnerable when it interfaces with the formal banking system, and this interface between the formal and informal sectors may also provide an opportunity for tackling the problem. Financial institutions should, for instance, be encouraged to develop more detailed understanding as to how alternative remittance and money value transfer systems utilise bank accounts to conduct their operations, particularly when accounts are used in the settlement process. They should also pay particular attention to the accounts that they suspect relate to underground banking operations – including foreign currency accounts and accounts held by trusts or offshore companies – whether or not the account holders are suspected of direct involvement in money laundering.

### 6.8.5 Restrictions on the Use of Cash

Cash-based economies are more prone to the increasing and undetected use of underground banking systems. It is therefore important to tackle the cash basis of the parallel economy by measures aimed at reducing the use of cash and, where necessary, improving the efficiency of the domestic banking system to make it more attractive. Where practical, salaries could be paid directly into bank accounts. Modern electronic methods of money management, such as the greater use of credit and debit cards, could be encouraged.

An effective intermediate step, however, might be to outlaw the use of cash payments for transactions above a certain size (Italy, for example, has taken this approach). Large transactions would therefore require the involvement of financial institutions. This would ensure that those involved in the transactions were subject to formal identification the transactions would be recorded, and the process would be subject to the money laundering controls applied to the formal economy.

Such an approach could be introduced gradually, beginning with a relatively high threshold, and gradually reducing it as the financial system developed in response to the opportunity that this would present.

## 6.9 Increasing Public Awareness

The offences and defences under the criminal law will generally need to apply to all citizens. This will equally apply to anti-money laundering legislation.

For example, it should be an offence for any natural or legal person to provide assistance to a criminal, to obtain, conceal, retain or invest funds that are the proceeds of criminal conduct. The penalties for committing such an offence without a reasonable excuse, for example that the person did not know or suspect anything or that they reported their knowledge at the earliest opportunity, can be significant.

However, in many countries where money laundering has been made a criminal offence, there is little public awareness of the reasons, the public responsibilities and the penalties for committing an offence. In addition, the responsibilities placed on financial institutions to identify their customers is generally not understood and will often cause inconvenience to genuine customers. Experience has shown that the measures will cause friction between the institutions and their customers if the underlying reasons and the social effects of not taking action have not been adequately explained.

To assist in persuading all citizens and institutions to play their part in the fight against crime and the laundering of the proceeds of crime, Commonwealth countries may wish to consider undertaking a public awareness raising campaign linked to the effects of crime on society. Criminal money in large amounts, such as that derived from drug trafficking, undermines the social, economic and political fabric of society and, consequently, affects the day-to-day life and environment of every citizen. A relatively crime-free society with a sound and effective criminal justice system provides a healthier and safer environment in which to live and work.

# 7

# Criminalising Money Laundering

## 7.1 Scope of the Criminal Offence of Money Laundering

Criminalising money laundering must be the starting point of any credible anti-money laundering strategy and it is now generally accepted that the international standard for a money laundering offence is one based on serious crimes
    FATF Recommendations 1–3 require that:

(i)   Countries should criminalise money laundering on the basis of the Vienna and Palermo Conventions.

(ii)  Countries should apply the crime of money laundering to all serious offences with a view to including the widest range of predicate offences, for example taking a threshold approach to all offences carrying a sentence of one year or more or which are punishable by a minimum penalty of six months of more.

(iii) As a minimum, a range of offences within each of the following designated categories of offences should be included:

- Participation in an organised criminal group and racketeering;

- Terrorism, including terrorist financing;

- Trafficking in human beings and migrant smuggling;

- Sexual exploitation, including sexual exploitation of children;

- Illicit trafficking in narcotic drugs and psychotropic substances;

- Illicit arms trafficking;

- Illicit trafficking in stolen and other goods;

- Corruption and bribery;

- Fraud;

- Counterfeiting currency;

- Counterfeiting and piracy of products;

- Environmental crime;

- Murder or grievous bodily injury;

- Kidnapping, illegal restraint and hostage-taking;

- Robbery or theft;

- Smuggling;

- Extortion;

- Forgery;

- Piracy; and

- Insider trading and market manipulation.

(iv) Predicate offences for money laundering should at least extend to offences committed in another country which constitutes an offence in that country and which would have constituted an offence if committed domestically.

(v) Criminal liability and/or civil or administrative liability should apply to legal persons as well as to individuals.

(vi) Legislative measures should include the power to identify, trace, freeze, seize and confiscate criminally obtained or laundered property.

## 7.2 The Elements of the Vienna Convention

The elements of the Vienna Convention laundering offence, together with illustrations of some of the forms they might take in practice, are set out below.

- **Conversion** – this would include the exchange of one currency for another or the exchange of cash for travellers cheques or other negotiable instruments or securities. It would cover the trading of securities. It could be taken to include the acceptance of cash or cheques for deposit in an account – converting the money into an accounting record.

- **Transfer** – this would cover any form of money transmission service, including wire transfer.

- **Concealment** – this might be taken to cover acceptance of deposits, and also activities such as the establishment of trusts or companies to hold assets.

- **Disguising the true nature, source, location, disposition, movement, rights with respect to, and/or ownership** – this is very similar to concealment, and would particularly include offshore trust and company formation activities.

- **Acquisition** – this might include the receipt of funds through correspondent accounts with other financial institutions, or acceptance as a trustee.

- **Possession** – again, this might cover holding funds on behalf of another party, particularly when there is a degree of discretion over the disposition of the funds.

- **Use** – this might cover discretionary investment of funds held for a client.

- **Participation, association, conspiracy, attempting, aiding, abetting, facilitating and/or counselling** – this might cover a wide range of advisory services, including investment advice and brokerage services.

## 7.3 The Elements of the Palermo Convention

The Palermo Convention established the requirement to combat four distinct areas of activity which are commonly used in support of transnational organised crime.

Under Article 5 participating in the activities of an 'organised criminal group' and 'organising, directing, aiding, abetting, facilitating or counselling' serious crimes involving organised criminal groups must be made offences.

Under Article 6 activities relating to 'money laundering' must be criminalised. This extends not only to cash but to any form of property which is the proceeds of crime, and includes any form of transfer or conversion of the property for the purpose of concealing its true origin. Simple acquisition or possession is also included if the person in possession knows that the property is the proceeds of crime.

Under Article 8 corruption must be criminalised where there is a link to transnational organised crime. These include offering, giving, soliciting and accepting any form of bribe, undue advantage or other inducement, where the proposed recipient is a public official and the purpose of the bribe relates to his or her official functions.

Under Article 23 participating states are required to criminalise any form of obstruction of justice, including the use of corrupt means (e.g. bribery or physical coercion) to influence testimony, other evidence or the actions of any law enforcement or other justice official.

Article 2 defines an 'organised criminal group' as one having:

- At least three members;

- The intention of taking action in concert for the purpose of committing a serious crime to derive a financial or other benefit;

- Some internal organisation or structure;

- Existed for some period of time before or after the actual commission of the offences involved.

Three protocols cover the specific crimes of:

- Trafficking in persons;

- Smuggling of migrants;

- Smuggling or illicit manufacture of firearms.

The provisions of the Convention which deal with extradition and mutual legal assistance are similar to provisions already in place in many regional or bilateral agreements. However, their significance is that the Convention is expected to be ratified by a large number of countries making legal assistance and extradition more widely available than previously.

Article 24 requires participating states to adopt appropriate measures to protect witnesses from potential intimidation or retaliation.

Articles 29 and 30 encourage the development of domestic training programmes and the provision of technical assistance to other less developed countries.

## 7.4 The Commonwealth Model Law

To assist Commonwealth countries to develop their national legislation, the Commonwealth Secretariat has produced a model law for the Prohibition of Money Laundering (known as 'the Model Law'). The Model Law is intended for use by common law countries and covers all of the issues addressed by the FATF Recommendations. An 'all serious crimes' money laundering offence was included.

Heads of Government, at their meeting in Auckland in November 1995, agreed that a common legislative approach would facilitate international co-operation and invited member states to draw benefit from the Model Law. The Model Law has been updated during 2003 to reflect the developing international standards.

## 7.5 The Inclusion of Economic Crimes within Money Laundering Offences

A number of countries have deregulated their economies in order to improve the efficiency of production and use of resources. However, the trend towards financial and economic deregulation has both a positive and a negative impact on the problems of economic crime. On the positive side, by removing the regulations and restrictions that are subject to abuse, certain forms of economic crime automatically fall away. For instance, it is impossible to have a crime of exchange control evasion if there are no exchange controls.

At the same time, deregulation brings freedoms that can be abused by criminals, particularly those involved in other forms of activity that remain as economic crimes, such as tax evasion and corruption. Many countries suffer from high levels of economic crime which hinder their efforts to achieve sustainable economic growth.

It is important therefore to consider:

- How any approaches to tackling money laundering can additionally be used to combat the laundering of the proceeds of economic crime; and

- What steps can be taken to monitor large inflows and outflows of capital/currency once regulations and restrictions are removed.

### 7.5.1 Tax Evasion

The inclusion of tax evasion within the predicate offences for the criminalisation of money laundering is clouded by the perception that tax evasion is a domestic crime as opposed to an internationally recognised serious crime such as drug trafficking.

Public attitudes towards tax evasion are complicated by the generally held view that the payment of tax is something to be avoided whenever possible. This view generates an ever-growing 'tax planning' industry, serving corporations and individuals (particularly wealthy individuals) and advising them on how to minimise their tax liabilities. This often involves running as close as possible to the line that separates what is legal – tax minimisation – from what is illegal – tax evasion.

While countries that include all serious crimes within the definition of money laundering do not place tax-related offences in a special category from other serious crimes, many countries have taken the decision specifically to exclude tax-related offences from their money laundering legislation. In some countries, tax offences are still subject to the money laundering legislation, but information that might relate to the laundering of the proceeds of fiscal offences is not passed to the revenue authorities until another criminal offence is proved. Other countries, however, have involved their revenue authorities directly in their anti-money laundering regimes, and can effectively offset some or all of the costs of their operations against recovered tax revenues as well as against the confiscated proceeds of other crimes.

Evidence shows that where tax evasion has become a normal activity within a particular country, the inclusion of tax evasion within the activities constituting serious crime can significantly improve government finances through increased levels of tax recovery.

### Tax Evasion as a Smokescreen

The lack of consistency in the treatment of tax evasion has provided an additional opportunity for the criminals. Money launderers involved in other crimes such as drug trafficking have frequently used tax reasons as a smokescreen for their unusual or abnormal transactions or instructions. In recognition of this growing practice. The interpretative note to FATF Recommendation 13 states that:

> In implementing Recommendation 13, suspicious transactions should be reported by financial institutions regardless of whether they are also thought to involve tax matters. Countries should take into account that, in order to deter financial institutions from reporting

*suspicious transactions, money launderers may seek to state inter alia that their transactions are related to tax matters.*

In addition FATF Recommendation 40 concerning international co-operation provides that:

*Exchanges (of information) should be permitted without unduly restrictive conditions. In particular:*

a) *Competent authorities should not refuse a request for assistance on the sole ground that the request is also considered to involve fiscal matters.*

## 7.6  Bribery and Corruption

Bribery and corruption raise problems of definition and ethics. In many countries the practice of offering bribes in order to obtain a contract or other advantage has become a normal part of business life. Likewise, public sector corruption, i.e. the abuse of public office for private gain has become endemic in some countries. Corruption damages development and the possibility of laundering the proceeds of corruption through the world's financial systems allows it to grow to a massively larger scale than would otherwise be possible. Significant international initiatives are now in place to tackle the problems of bribery and corruption.

### 7.6.1 The OECD Bribery Convention

One of the major international achievements has been the conclusion of the OECD Convention on the bribery of foreign public officials in the course of international business transactions (the OECD Bribery Convention). Specifically, the Convention provides that the making or receiving of a bribe should be made a criminal offence and provides for the seizure of the bribe or the proceeds of the bribe.

### 7.6.2 Grand Corruption

Corruption has been defined by the world bank as 'the abuse of public office for private gain'. Transparency International defines it as 'the abuse of entrusted power for private gain'. Whatever the definition, corruption invariably taints reputations and practices, infects political processes and economic stability, and generally deprives one person or group of persons to the benefit of another person or interest.

Corruption is not only a major disincentive to healthy economies growth, but it is also a major disincentive to outside investment and long term aid.[4]

The corrupt diversion of government funds and international aid money has become a significant problem for some Commonwealth countries and for many countries steps to combat corruption have become a prerequisite for contained international support. Corrupt government officials generally wish to place the proceeds form their corrupt acts beyond the sight and reach of their own home jurisdictions. The illegally diverted funds concerned are generally laundered through bank accounts, companies or trusts set up in other countries or offshore financial centres. Most financial institutions do not willingly seek to acquire such funds, and many are increasingly refusing to accept them if they are identifiable. The criminal and civil liabilities for banks and others who knowingly or unwittingly launder the proceeds can be significant in addition to the reputational risks.

Financial institutions that know their customers and the sources of their wealth and income can usually be expected to recognise abnormal financial flows and could be expected to become suspicious of the large financial flows generated by corrupt payments. Those funds can then be reported to the relevant authorities and the process of returning them can commence. However, difficulties arise in practice when the financial institution does not know that a foreign customer is a public sector official with potential access to substantial government funds. While there may be no doubt in relation to heads of state and other very prominent individuals, many will not be recognisable as such.

Commonwealth countries that are vulnerable to high levels of corruption or diverted aid funds may therefore consider maintaining a list of individuals who fall in this category. This could then be made available to international banks through their supervisory bodies and would permit all banks to monitor the accounts of political customers or family members and assist in the reporting of transactions that might be linked to corruption.

## 7.7 Secrecy versus Confidentiality

Banking confidentiality is widely recognised as playing a legitimate role in protecting the confidentiality of the financial affairs of individuals and legal entities.

This right derives from the general principle of privacy and the concept that the relationship between a banker and his customer obliges a bank to treat all its customers' affairs as confidential. All countries provide, to a greater or lesser extent, the authority and obligation for banks to refuse to disclose customer information to ordinary third parties.

In common law countries, the circumstances when the common law duty of confidentiality between a financial institution and its customers may be breached are set out in the Tournier decision (*Tournier v National Provincial and Union Bank of England 1924*). The three most important of these circumstances in the context of money laundering are:

- when the bank is required by law to breach confidence;

- when breach of confidence is necessary in the bank's own interests; and

- when breach of confidence is in the legitimate public interest.

Money laundering legislation normally defines circumstances under which a financial institution is required to disclose information to a designated authority and the financial institution is therefore protected from suit for breach of confidentiality by the need to disclose under compulsion of law.

Where banking confidentiality is enshrined in statute, it may be necessary to ensure that money laundering legislation provides adequate gateways (with appropriate checks and balances) through the confidentiality provisions to permit the disclosure of suspicions. Most confidentiality legislation permits financial institutions to pass on knowledge of criminal activity to the authorities coupled with explicit statutory protection from breach of customer confidentiality.

However, some Commonwealth countries extend customer confidentiality beyond the common law right, to the statutory right to secrecy. In these cases, legislation will usually provide that banks and other financial institutions must keep information concerning their affairs secret. Any person who discloses information relating to the identity, assets, liabilities, transactions and accounts of a customer will commit a criminal offence.

To be effective, money laundering legislation must allow financial institutions to pass on their knowledge and their suspicions of money laundering to the relevant authorities. The continued existence of banking secrecy legislation, rather than merely a customer's right to confidentiality, will prohibit the development of an effective anti-money laundering strategy.

Commonwealth countries should also be aware that if banking secrecy legislation prohibits disclosure of customer information in response to a Foreign Court Order or a US subpoena in respect of a criminal investigation, that country will be officially classified by the FATF as a non co-operative jurisdiction (see Chapter 4, section 4.4).

## 7.8 Implementing a Requirement to Report Knowledge/Suspicion of Money Laundering

In order for a national strategy to succeed, it is essential that financial institutions and professional firms (and within them, individual members of staff) are required, by statute, to report any knowledge or suspicion of money laundering.

### 7.8.1 Determining Reporting Requirements

The FATF Recommendations recognise two different approaches to the task of reporting.

Firstly, institutions should be required to report knowledge or suspicion of money laundering related to specific customer or transactions; this is known as suspicious transaction or suspicious activity reporting. FATF Recommendation 13 states:

*If a financial institution suspects or has reasonable grounds to suspect that funds are the proceeds of criminal activity or are related to terrorist financing, it should be required directly by law or regulation to report promptly its suspicions to the Financial Intelligence Unit (FIU).*

The inclusion of the words 'or has reasonable grounds to suspect' introduces into Recommendation 13 a new objective test of suspicion. This enhanced requirement is discussed in greater detail in Chapter 12.

Secondly, institutions can be required to undertake routine reporting of transactions above a specified threshold; this is known as currency transaction reporting. FATF Recommendation 19b states:

*Countries should consider the feasibility and utility of a system, where banks and other financial institutions and intermediaries would report all domestic and international currency transactions above a fixed amount to a national central agency with a computerised data base, available to competent authorities for use in money laundering or terrorist financing cases, subject to strict safeguards to ensure proper use of information.*

## 7.8.2 Suspicious Transaction/Activity Reporting

The idea that financial institutions should spontaneously report to the authorities, transactions that they have conducted merely because they are suspicious of those transactions or consider them to be unusual is perhaps the most radical element of the approach to combat money laundering. It often runs counter to other legislative/contractual commitments and counter to the natural instincts of most financial institutions, which place very strong emphasis on customer confidentiality.

### Why Should Financial Institutions Report Suspicious Transactions or Activity?

Where Recommendation 13 has been adopted, financial institutions, professional firms and other designated businesses will commit an offence if they do not report their suspicions of money laundering. However, there are two other reasons why financial institutions should co-operate in combating money laundering by disclosing details of suspicious transactions.

The first, is essentially a moral one. Regulated financial institutions and professional firms in particular are expected to be 'good citizens' who have a duty to uphold the law, and this duty may at times override the duty of confidentiality that they owe to their customers, if there is legitimate suspicion of wrong-doing. This issue of confidentiality is discussed in more detail below.

The second reason, for any financial or non-financial business to report suspicious transactions is that of simple self-interest – protecting themselves from fraud and protecting their reputation. The basis of trust on which the financial and professional systems operate can easily be undermined by the involvement of financial institutions or professional firms in criminal activity, even if the involvement was unintentional.

Any financial institution or professional firm that discovers it is holding criminal proceeds may be subject to criminal penalties under the common law (as an aider or abettor) or to a civil suit for constructive trust, even in the absence of money laundering legislation. By disclosing its situation to the authorities, a financial institution will to put itself in a safer position.

The options for establishing a central agency to receive and evaluate the suspicion reports is set out in section 9.1.

### 7.8.3 Protection for the Reporting Institution

While the legal situation protects reporting institutions from civil action by clients or criminal liability for breach of confidence, it does not protect staff from reprisals if the fact that a disclosure has been made becomes known to the customer. This possibly becomes significantly more acute if the report is made direct to the law enforcement agencies from the member of staff who is handling the transaction.

In some countries, legislation requires the identification of a senior manager within the institution who will be given responsibility for considering all 'suspicions', deciding if they should be passed to the authorities, and generally controlling the institution's reporting procedures. This role is often referred to as 'the Money Laundering Officer'.

### 7.8.4 Currency Transaction Reporting

Under a CTR regime, financial institutions report any transaction or transfer of funds above a fixed threshold to a central agency. This information is then put on a database and made available to investigators.

CTR regimes can impose significant compliance costs on financial institutions and their customers and, if the reporting threshold is set at an inappropriate level, can lead to the agency to which the reports are being sent being overloaded with information. This in turn will prevent the ability to analyses the information such that the money laundering transactions can be identified. However, from the government viewpoint, a well-run CTR system can potentially cover its costs. If resources and expertise were available to establish and maintain a computer-based CTR system, and the data was made available to revenue authorities to use to pursue tax evasion, this might be an attractive option for some Commonwealth governments.

A CTR system is often deemed to prove helpful in three situations:

- Where it is considered that the quality and educational standards of many staff, or the standard of the systems, within financial institutions are insufficient to exercise and apply the judgement necessary in a suspicion-based reporting regime. This may be considered a short-term phenomenon, and implementing a routine CTR system may be an expedient starting point (legislation permitting);

- As a first step in monitoring and reporting. With money laundering, one of the choke points is at the point of conversion of notes into instruments (cheques, money transfer orders, etc.), with the most likely being the conversion of convertible currencies. Therefore, in the early stages of a strategy, the routine reporting of convertible currency transactions (thus excluding the more numerous domestic currency transactions) may be an effective option;

- The application of money laundering legislation to tax evasion and other forms of economic crime has the potential to improve government finances through increased levels of tax recovery. Where the fiscal benefits are potentially very high, there is scope for the introduction of a CTR system.

**Often the most effective anti-money laundering regimes require both CTR and suspicion-based reporting, but CTR alone has been found to be ineffective.**

### 7.8.5 *Reporting International Capital/Currency Movements*

While deregulation and liberalisation of the financial system requires the removal of controls and restrictions over the 'free' flow of currency and capital, many jurisdictions maintain or implement a reporting procedure to permit the ongoing monitoring of such movements. Financial institutions may be requested to report to the central bank all movements of capital/currency, over a specified financial threshold, in to and out of the country. Such a reporting procedure serves two purposes:

- It provides the central bank with essential statistics and information in respect of the balance of payments, etc.; and

- It provides the central bank with the opportunity to recognise any unusual flows of capital/currency (by size, source or destination) which may be suspicious and warrant further enquiry.

# 8

# Setting Obligations for the Financial Sector, the Professions and Other Designated Businesses

## 8.1 General Requirements

While the basic statutory money laundering offences and defences, e.g. the requirement not to assist any other person to launder the proceeds of crime, will apply universally, additional measures are necessary to strengthen the financial institutions, non-financial businesses and professions against abuse by money launderers.

FATF Recommendations 4–15 set out the measures to be taken by financial institutions covering:

- customer due diligence

- record keeping

- special attention to complex and large transactions

- reporting suspicions

- development of policies, procedures and controls including the screening of employees, employee training and an audit programme to test the system.

Recommendation 16 applies the financial institution requirements to all designated non-financial businesses and professions, subject only to an exemption when the information was obtained in circumstances covered by legal professional privilege (Recommendation 13).

Recommendations 17–19 include a number of other measures to deter money laundering and terrorist financing:

- The imposition of sanctions for non-compliance;

- The prohibition of dealings with shell banks;

- Measures to detect or monitor cross border transfers of cash or bearer instruments.

Recommendation 20 encourages countries to apply the FATF recommendations to a wider range of businesses that may pose a money laundering or terrorist financing risk.

Recommendation 20 also encourages the development of non-cash based methods of payment and money management.

Recommendation 21 requires financial institutions and other designated professions and businesses to give special attention to relationships and transactions with countries that have material deficiencies in their anti-money laundering and terrorist strategies.

The recommendation also states that the institutions, businesses and professions should apply their policies and procedures to subsidiaries and branches located abroad.

## 8.2 Defining the Scope of Financial Sector Activities

The following activities to be covered as a minimum are set out in the Glossary to the FATF Recommendations:

1. Acceptance of deposits and other repayable funds from the public;[5]

2. Lending;[6]

3. Financial Leasing;[7]

4. The transfer of money or value;[8]

5. Issuing and managing means of payment (e.g. credit and debit cards, cheques, traveller's cheques, money orders and bankers' drafts, electronic money);

6. Financial guarantees and commitments;

7. Trading in
   (a) money market instruments (cheques, bills, CDs, derivatives etc.)
   (b) foreign exchange
   (c) exchange, interest rate and index instruments
   (d) transferable securities
   (e) commodity futures trading;

8. Participation in securities issues and the provision of financial services related to such issues;

9. Individual and collective portfolio management;

10. Safekeeping and administration of cash or liquid securities on behalf of other persons;

11. Otherwise investing, administering or managing funds or money on behalf of other persons;

12. Underwriting and placement of life insurance and other investment related insurance;[9]

13. Money and currency changing.

Beyond the traditional banking sector, there is no general definition of financial institution. It is therefore important that each Commonwealth country defines the scope of its financial sector broadly enough to cover all the types of financial activity that might be considered particularly at risk from being used by money launderers.

For example, in most countries there is a class of persons that provide financial advice or planning services to the public. These services often entail the investment adviser examining a client's financial needs and recommending financial products and services to meet those needs. In some countries, advisers who provide advice on certain types of investments, for example pensions, life insurance, or unit trusts, must be authorised and abide by rules to protect customers and investors. However, depending on the country concerned, financial planning or advice may also be offered not only by specific authorised investment advisers, but also by lawyers, accountants or other types of professionals. It may be that the adviser also offers other types of advice, in areas such as tax planning or purchasing foreign real estate.

The recommendation for defining a financial institution covers a wide variety of financial activities, including the provision of various investment services for a client whereby the financial institution handles and invests the client's money or funds. This should extend to the provision of investment advice, where it is linked to handling client funds. However, it would not automatically include advisers or entities that only provide advice and which do not themselves handle the client's funds. Given that investment advisers occupy an important role as financial intermediaries, and are often particularly well placed to know the client's affairs, consideration should be given as to whether they would be subject to AML obligations, even where they do not handle the client's funds.

Several of the relevant financial sector activities listed in 8.2 above may be conducted outside the formal financial sector, for example by unlicensed cash remitters, bureaux de change and in some cases casinos. It is important that all those conducting relevant activities are covered by the financial sector regulations.

### 8.2.1 Displacement

Experience indicates that where money laundering legislation is applied only to part of the financial sector, laundering activity quickly shifts into those areas where the legislation does not apply. This process is known as displacement. In particular, the activity will often be displaced from the formal financial sector into the informal sector and parallel economy (see Chapter 6). Displacement will also occur out of the financial sector into other areas such as retailing, arts or antiques, where cash is accepted in settlement. The scope of anti-money laundering regulation must therefore be kept under review and the requirements extend to other business sectors as the need arises.

## 8.3 Determining the Scope and Vulnerability of Non-financial Sector Businesses and Professions

The FATF Recommendations designate the following non-financial businesses and professions as being vulnerable to money laundering and terrorist financing:

(a) Casinos – when customers engage in financial transactions equal to or above the applicable designated threshold;

(b) Real estate agents – when they are involved in transactions for their client concerning the buying and selling of real estate;

(c) Dealers in precious metals and dealers in precious stones – when they engage in any cash transaction with a customer equal to or above the applicable designated threshold;

(d) Lawyers, notaries, other independent legal professionals and accountants when they prepare for or carry out transactions for their client concerning the following activities

- buying and selling of real estate

- managing of client money, securities or other assets

- management of bank, savings or securities accounts

- organisation of contributions for the creation, operation or management of companies

- creation, operation of management of legal persons of arrangements, and buying and selling of business entities.

(e) Trust and company service providers when they prepare for or carry out transactions for a client concerning the activities listed in the definition in the Glossary.

The Basle paper on customer due diligence for banks also identifies client accounts opened by professional intermediaries as a high-risk area. These concerns have caused the Offshore Group of Banking Supervisors to set up a working group made up of members of the group and representatives from several other countries and relevant international organisations. This group is working to produce a recommended statement of minimum standards and/or guidance for trust and company service providers.

The risks associated with 'gatekeepers' have also been recognised by the G-8. Following the meeting of Justice Ministers in Moscow in 1999, the official communiqué noted that many money laundering schemes involve misuse of financial intermediaries. The Ministers noted that they would 'consider requiring or enhancing suspicious transaction reporting by the "gatekeepers" to the international financial system, including company formation agents, accounts, auditors and lawyers …'.

### 8.3.1 Casinos and Other Gambling Businesses

Casinos are vulnerable to manipulation by money launderers due to the fast-paced and cash intensive nature of the games and because casinos provide their customers with a wide array of financial services. Financial services available at casinos are similar and, in many cases, identical to those generally provided by banks and other depository institutions, and can include customer deposit or credit accounts, facilities for transmitting and receiving funds transfers directly from other institutions, and cheque cashing and currency exchange services.

Evidence suggests that the gambling environment often attracts criminal elements involved in a variety of illicit activities, including fraud, narcotics trafficking and money laundering. With large volumes of currency being brought in and played by legitimate customers, gaming can create a good 'cover' for money launderers who are in possession of large amounts of currency. Casinos are also attractive to organised crime if the criminals are able to take over and control the casino, thus providing them with an opportunity to launder their illicit proceeds, as well as engage in other types of criminality.

The money laundering schemes that have been uncovered include instances where casinos were used by individuals to commit offences including structuring of transactions and money laundering. Many of these schemes involved organised crime. Money launderers have also been known to use agents to disguise the true ownership of the funds and are willing to lose some of the money while gambling as a necessary cost of doing business. Other techniques include:

- Buying chips or tokens with cash, conducting minimal betting and then requesting repayment by a cheque drawn on the casino's account;

- Using a chain of casinos with establishments in different countries and asking for the amount held by the casino in credit for a gambler to be made available in another jurisdiction and then withdraw it in the form of a cheque there;

- Asking for winners' cheques to be made out in the name of third persons.

A casino must know its customer to make an informed decision as to whether a transaction is suspicious. Many casinos already know a great deal about their customers from information routinely obtained through deposit, credit, cheque cashing and player rating accounts. These accounts generally require casinos to obtain basic identification information about the account holders and to inquire into the kinds of wagering activities in which the customer is likely to engage. For example, deposit and credit accounts track customer deposits and casino extensions of credit. The player rating account tracks gaming activity and is designed primarily to award complimentary perquisites to volume players, and to serve as a marketing tool to identify frequent customers and to encourage continued patronage. In certain instances, casinos use credit bureaux to verify information obtained from customers. All of these sources of information can help a casino to better understand its customer base and to evaluate specific transactions that appear to lack justification or otherwise cannot be explained as falling within the usual methods of legitimate business.

Other than casinos, the most prevalent forms of legal gambling include horse racing betting (on and off course), slot and other gaming machines, soccer and other types of sports betting, spread betting, card clubs, and lotteries and pool competitions. Some of these other types of gambling provide an ideal cover for money launderers because they have a high volume cash turnover, offer considerable anonymity for customers, have no recognisable audit trail and usually welcome persons that engage in significant gambling. The vulnerabilities identified above for casinos apply equally to some other forms of gambling. In addition, in some jurisdictions gambling businesses such as betting shops, card clubs and off-course bookmakers are vulnerable to money laundering because they provide services similar to those provided by financial institutions, including customer deposit or credit accounts, facilities for transmitting and receiving funds from other financial institutions, cheque cashing and currency exchange.

Gambling is particularly attractive to money launderers at the placement stage. Sale of winning horse-racing tickets has been identified in money laundering cases, with the criminal buying winning tickets with criminal proceeds and then obtaining a cheque when the winning ticket is returned. There is evidence that telephone betting accounts have been abused by launderers both as a means of disguising who is really gambling and also legitimising funds; cash is paid into such accounts, a small amount is gambled and the balance transferred back out into a bank account. The bank then records the source of the funds as winnings, thereby lessening suspicion.

Gambling businesses that use a token or chip system, such as poker machines, are also vulnerable to money laundering. Any chip system that permits a customer to purchase chips with funds which can then be sold back provides a low cost, intensive opportunity for structuring and conversion of funds.

Historically, organised crime and other criminal elements have always been attracted to gambling. The combination of large profits, cash transactions and the opportunity to launder funds attracts criminal operators. The large amounts of cash introduced daily by legitimate customers provide cover for money launderers without necessarily alerting the authorities.

### 8.3.2 Real Estate Agents

A recent FATF study into money laundering methods, techniques and trends found that:

> *The real estate sector is now fully within the sphere of money laundering activities. Investment of illicit capital in real estates is a classic and proven method of laundering dirty money.*

In considering the application of anti-money laundering measures to the real estate industry, one must take into account that this sector may vary considerably in its types of clients, and the types and value of transactions that real estate agents conduct. However, some practical difficulties might arise in applying anti-money laundering measures to such businesses and activities, mainly due to the traditional lack of specific regulation or control by a supervisory authority.

Where money laundering risks are mitigated by the fact that the client is usually the vendor rather than the purchaser, where the real estate agent does not generally handle the client's funds or other assets, and when the transactions will be subject to scrutiny by other intermediaries such as lawyers, banks or mortgage lenders, the risks can be considered to be low. In such cases a light touch approach to regulatory and compliance requirements might be appropriate.

### 8.3.3 Dealers in High-value Goods

The FATF typologies reports have identified sellers of high-value objects such as works of art as having a significant presence in laundering activities. Gold dealers have also been identified as being vulnerable to money laundering in that anti-money laundering measures targeting the traditional financial sector have caused customers wishing to purchase bullion anonymously to turn to other sources.

The 1998–99 FATF *Typologies Report* also identified close links between wholesale and retail dealing in gold, informal remittance systems and money laundering cases. Similar links have also been found between money laundering and trade in diamonds. More recently, these industries have been linked to the financing of terrorist organisations and activities.

In a number of FATF and other countries, there has also been extensive use of luxury vehicles such as expensive automobiles, and boats or planes, as part of the money laundering process. Such items are used both at the placement level, as a means of transporting cash or other criminal proceeds, as well as at the layering and integration stages, when they are luxury items that criminals own as part of their assets. Another type of business that is subject to anti-money laundering obligations in several countries and which is involved in transporting cash and high value items are professional carriers of cash and other valuables.

As with estate agents, dealers in high-value goods will vary significantly in the nature of their clients and the value of their transactions. Practical difficulties in applying anti-money laundering controls may arise because of the lack of a formal regulatory or supervisory structure. One answer might be to impose a compulsory transaction reporting requirement coupled with an identification requirement for transactions over a given limit. An amount equivalent to US$10,000 either for single of linked transactions might be appropriate.

### 8.3.4 Trust and Company Service Providers

The FATF has consistently found that legal entities or other types of legal relationships (such as trusts), usually formed and managed by professional service providers, are a common feature of money laundering schemes. A major part of the problem is the lack of transparency concerning the beneficial ownership and control of corporate vehicles such as companies, trusts, foundations etc., but an equally important issue is addressing the risks posed by the professionals that create and manage these vehicles.

Companies and trusts are often used by money launderers and other criminals who wish to conceal their identity. For example, as stated in the 2001 *Typologies Report*, FATF experts found that 'trusts, along with various forms of corporate entities, are increasingly perceived as an important element of large-scale or complex money laundering schemes'. Because of this, it is important to ensure that those who are responsible for forming and administering trusts and companies must themselves know the identity of the persons who are the beneficiaries or beneficial owners, respectively, and who effectively control the trust or company in question. In 2000, the FATF examined the role of the individuals or agents that help to create such entities, and found them to be a key factor in an increasing number of complex money laundering schemes.

The need to take action with respect to trust and company service providers has also been recognised by other international bodies. An OECD report has highlighted the role that trust and company service providers can play in the misuse of corporate vehicles. The identified misuse is not restricted to money laundering, but extends to bribery and corruption, hiding assets from legitimate creditors and claimants, fraud, securities law and tax offences. The report states:

> *Corporate service providers regularly design structures to ensure that the beneficial owner remains anonymous, and often act as the intermediary between the client and the authorities in the jurisdiction of incorporation …*

> *Trustees may also play a role in obscuring the identity of the beneficial owner …*

There is a wide range of different types of businesses or professionals that act as professional service providers for the creation and administration of companies, trusts, foundations and other legal entities or arrangements. For example, in many jurisdictions, lawyers and accountants play an important role in this type of business, but the service is also provided by banks, businesses that specialise in providing these services or suitably qualified individuals or partnerships. The same term can also have different meanings in different jurisdictions. In some jurisdictions, a trust company is a company whose business is acting as a trust service provider, i.e. it forms and administers trusts and arranges for the appointment of or acts as trustee. In others, a trust company may also be entitled to do banking business or provide similar services with respect to companies. What counts for anti-money laundering purposes is not the name of business that provides the service but the types of service it provides. The services that should be covered are:

- Acting as a formation agent of legal persons;

- Acting as (or arranging for another person to act as) a director or secretary of a company, a partner of a partnership, or a similar position in relation to other legal persons;

- Providing a registered office, business address or accommodation, correspondence or administrative address for a company, a partnership or any other legal person or arrangement;

- Acting as (or arranging for another person to act as) a trustee of an express trust;

- Acting as (or arranging for another person to act as) a nominee shareholder for another person.

When considering the options for including these services within an anti-money laundering strategy, it is important to bear in mind the need for a level playing field and the displacement effect that occurs when measures are taken in one jurisdiction but not in another. In relation to trust and company service providers, there is evidence that service providers relocate from jurisdictions that have adopted strong anti-money laundering and regulatory measures to those that have no such measures. Another important general consideration is that trust and company service providers often control large amounts of client funds and can make investment decisions for the trusts and companies that they control, thus acting in a comparable way to investment or portfolio managers. This has implications for anti-money laundering controls, but also for protection of customers against criminal activity or incompetence by the service provider.

### 8.3.5 Lawyers, Notaries and Legal Professionals

Since the FATF first commenced studying money laundering methods and techniques on a systematic basis in 1995–96, lawyers have been consistently mentioned in FATF typologies reports as being linked to money laundering schemes and cases. A variety of reasons have been cited as to why lawyers appear to be frequently involved in money laundering:

- It has been commonly observed that criminals use lawyers' client accounts for the placement and layering of funds. In many counties, this offers the advantage to the launderer of the protection that is afforded by legal professional privilege or professional secrecy;

- In a number of countries, lawyers provide a service as a 'gatekeeper', that is, through their specialised expertise they are able to create the corporate vehicles, trusts and other legal arrangements that facilitate money laundering;

- Lawyers offer the financial advice that is a required element of complex money laundering schemes;

- The use of lawyers and the corporate entities they create can provide the criminal with a veneer of respectability for the money laundering operations.

In addition, it has been uniformly observed by the international organisations that as anti-money laundering controls are effectively implemented in the financial sector, money launderers are turning to other sectors, including the use of professionals, to launder their illegal proceeds. For example, the involvement (unknowingly and otherwise) of lawyers and other professionals in money laundering cases is frequently noted in the 1998 Report of the UN Office for Drug Control and Crime Prevention on financial havens, banking secrecy and money laundering.

The particular role, history and status of the legal profession and the rules that attach to it mean that very careful attention will need to be given when considering the application of anti-money laundering obligations to such professionals. In particular, due to the professional secrecy or privilege that exists in relation to certain types of communications with clients, the application of the requirement to report suspicious transactions will need to be closely examined. Professional secrecy or privilege is a principle that exists in all members, but its precise boundaries vary, depending on the structure of the relevant legal system. The objective is to make it more difficulty for actual or potential money launderers to attempt to misuse the services of the lawyer, while still taking into account fundamental rights.

### 8.3.6 Accountants

As with lawyers, over recent years FATF studies of money laundering methods and techniques have linked accountants to money laundering schemes and cases, and accountants appear to be involved in money laundering for reasons similar to those applicable to lawyers:

- In a number of countries, accountants act as 'gatekeepers' – through their specialised expertise they are able to create the corporate vehicles, trusts and other legal arrangements that facilitate money laundering;

- Accountants offer financial and fiscal advise that is often a required element of complex money laundering schemes;

- The use of accountants and the corporate entities they create can provide the criminal with a veneer of respectability for their money laundering operations;

- As anti-money laundering controls are effectively implemented in the financial sector, money launderers are turning to other sectors, including the use of professionals to launder their illegal proceeds.

The role that is played by external accountants as 'gatekeepers', whether knowingly or otherwise, and the risks that might result if they are acting for criminal clients is well established. In addition, accountants acting as auditors also have a very important role, since they are the professionals responsible for checking financial statements, verifying the accuracy of books and records and checking on various types of controls for companies and businesses globally. Internal auditors working in financial institutions often already have a significant role in combating money laundering and in checking the internal controls that exist within the organisation. Similarly, external auditors could, in certain circumstances be well placed to perform checks on the adequacy of measures in place in the businesses in which they are conducting an audit. Other types of external accounting professionals, such as those engaged in forensic accounting or risk management, could also make important contributions to combating money laundering.

Again, as with the legal profession, the particular role and history of the accounting profession, and particularly external auditors (who are often performing a statutory function), mean that very careful attention will need to be given when considering the application of anti-money laundering obligations to such professionals. In particular, careful consideration will need to be given to auditors' obligations concerning the reporting of illegal activity, the rules of confidentiality or professional secrecy that apply in relation to certain types of documents or communications with clients, and the interaction with the application of the requirement to report suspicious transactions. An external auditor usually has a statutory obligation to assist the board of a company and its shareholders to assess if the financial statements of the company are true and correct. In some countries, this role and function means that in certain circumstances an auditor is subject to professional secrecy obligations.

## 8.4 Regulations for Financial Institutions, Professions and Other Designated Businesses

As stated in section 8.1 above, specific regulations for financial institutions, the professions and other designated businesses are required to underpin the general criminal law. The regulations should require the financial institutions, professions and businesses concerned to establish and maintain specific policies and procedures to guard against their businesses and the financial system being used for money laundering.

### 8.4.1 The Purpose and Scope of the Regulations

In essence, the financial, professional and business sector regulations are designed to achieve two purposes: firstly to enable suspicious transactions to be recognised as such and reported to the authorities; and secondly to ensure that if a customer comes under investigation in the future, a financial institution can provide its part of the audit trail.

To comply with the FATF Recommendations, the requirements should cover:

- The implementation of policies and controls;

- Identification and 'know your customer' procedures;

- Record-keeping requirements;

- Measures for the recognition of suspicious transactions;

- Reporting procedures for suspicious transactions and possibly currency transaction reporting;

- Awareness raising, education and training of relevant staff.

When determining controls and procedures, and indeed when drafting legislation, it is essential that supervisory authorities bear in mind that relatively simple requirements which are easy to fulfil are much more likely to be accepted and followed than cumbersome requirements which place excessive demands on businesses and their staff. Wherever possible, the requirements should simply be an extension of the due diligence already practised within the financial, professional or business sector.

## 8.4.2 The Implementation of Policies and Controls

A sound anti-money laundering and crime prevention strategy must emanate from board and senior management level. Senior management should therefore be made fully accountable for their institution's compliance with the AML requirements.

While the Board must retain collective responsibility for setting overall policy and compliance, it is generally found to be valuable for the Board to appoint one member of senior management as the central point of contact with the authorities, particularly in respect of the reporting of suspicious transactions. This person is generally referred to as the money laundering reporting officer (MLRO) and, depending on the size of the institution, may also be responsible for overall anti-money laundering compliance.

To ensure that the Board does not abdicate its collective responsibility for compliance to the MLRO, or some other designated person, it can be useful to require relevant businesses to prepare an annual report setting out how they have met their anti-money laundering obligations, including the requirement to report suspicions. These annual reports can then be made available to supervisors and other regulators as and when required.

## 8.4.3 Customer Due Diligence – Establishing Identification and 'Know Your Customer' Procedures

FATF Recommendation 5 states that:[10]

*Financial institutions should not keep anonymous accounts or accounts in obviously fictitious names.*

*Financial institutions should undertake customer due diligence measures, including identifying and verifying the identity of their customers, when:*

- *establishing business relations;*

- *carrying out occasional transactions: (i) above the applicable designated threshold; or (ii) that are wire transfers in the circumstances covered by the Interpretative Note to Special Recommendation VII;*

- there is a suspicion of money laundering or terrorist financing; or

- the financial institution has doubts about the veracity or adequacy of previously obtained customer identification data.

The customer due diligence (CDD) measures to be taken are as follows:

a) Identifying the customer and verifying that customer's identity using reliable, independent source documents, data or information.

b) Identifying the beneficial owner, and taking reasonable measures to verify the identity of the beneficial owner such that the financial institution is satisfied that it knows who the beneficial owner is. For legal persons and arrangements this should include financial institutions taking reasonable measures to understand the ownership and control structure of the customer.

c) Obtaining information on the purpose and intended nature of the business relationship.

d) Conducting ongoing due diligence on the business relationship and scrutiny of transactions undertaken throughout the course of that relationship to ensure that the transactions being conducted are consistent with the institution's knowledge of the customer, their business and risk profile, including, where necessary, the source of funds.

Financial institutions should apply each of the CDD measures under (a) to (d) above, but may determine the extent of such measures on a risk sensitive basis depending on the type of customer, business relationship or transaction. The measures that are taken should be consistent with any guidelines issued by competent authorities. For higher risk categories, financial institutions should perform enhanced due diligence. In certain circumstances, where there are low risks, countries may decide that financial institutions can apply reduced or simplified measures.

Financial institutions should verify the identity of the customer and beneficial owner before or during the course of establishing a business relationship or conducting transactions for occasional customers. Countries may permit financial institutions to complete the verification as soon as reasonably practicable following the establishment of the relationship, where the money laundering risks are effectively managed and where this is essential not to interrupt the normal conduct of business.

Where the financial institution is unable to comply with paragraphs (a) to (c) above, it should not open the account, commence business relations or perform the transaction; or should terminate the business relationship; and should consider making a suspicious transactions report in relation to the customer.

These requirements should apply to all new customers, though financial institutions should also apply this Recommendation to existing customers on the basis of materiality and risk, and should conduct due diligence on such existing relationships at appropriate times.

Recommendation 10 contains the following record-keeping requirements for customer identification evidence:

> *Financial Institutions should keep records on the identification data obtained through the customer due diligence process (eg copies or records of official identification documents like passports, identity cards, driving licenses or similar documents), account files and business correspondence for at least five years after the business relationship is ended.*

## The Purpose of Customer Due Diligence Procedures

Customer due diligence, i.e. 'knowing your customer' serves two purposes. The first is to provide an audit trail for investigators pursuing money laundering operations. If financial transactions can be linked to individual account holders, it is possible for law enforcement authorities to put together an effective case when they wish to prosecute criminals and confiscate the proceeds of their crimes. Every failure to seek and record true identity makes it easier for criminals to retain their money.

Effective customer due diligence procedures serve a second purpose, in that they will make it difficult for criminals to use financial institutions. Where individuals are required to provide evidence of their identity and the purpose and background to the relationship, criminals have the choice of:

- Having their true identity recorded (which leaves them open to greater risk of capture, conviction and confiscation); or

- Using false identification documentation (which may be spotted by staff in financial institutions, leading again to capture and conviction); or

- Using intermediaries to conduct the transactions or open the accounts on their behalf (which raises the costs and increases the risks of detection).

Extending the customer due diligence requirements beyond the financial sector will remove the alternative for determined launderers to use non-financial institutions as gatekeepers to the financial system.

Experience in many countries has been that the introduction of identification, 'know your customer' and record-keeping procedures, has benefited financial institutions. The requirement to identify their customers and to know their business has empowered the institutions to obtain information that assists them in their risk management procedures, without deterring customers who now know that they would be asked the same questions in any other institution. At the same time, legitimate customers who are aware of the legal responsibilities placed on financial institutions and other relevant businesses are more willing to provide information to the institutions. Knowing enough about customers and their legitimate business activities forms the basis for recognising suspicious arrangements and transactions.

## Simplified or Reduced Customer Due Diligence Measures

Historically most EU member states have permitted financial institutions certain concessions with respect to verifying the identity of customers seeking to enter into business relationships.

The FATF Recommendations now recognise this concept as stated in the following interpretative note to Recommendation 5.

*The general rule is that customers must be subject to the full range of CDD measures, including the requirement to identify the beneficial owner. Nevertheless there are circumstances where the risk of money laundering or terrorist financing is lower, where information on the identity of the customer and the beneficial owner of a customer is publicly available, or where adequate checks and controls exist elsewhere in national systems. In such circumstances it could be reasonable for a country to allow its financial institutions to apply simplified or reduced CDD measures when identifying and verifying the identity of the customer and the beneficial owner.*

*Examples of customers where simplified or reduced CDD measures could apply are:*

- *Financial Institutions – where they are subject to requirements to combat money laundering and terrorist financing consistent with the FATF Recommendations and are supervised for compliance with those controls.*

- *Public companies that are subject to regulatory disclosure requirements.*

- *Government administrations or enterprises.*

*Simplified or reduced CDD measures could also apply to the beneficial owners of pooled accounts held by designated non-financial businesses or professions, provided that those businesses or professions are subject to requirements to combat money laundering and terrorist financing consistent with the FATF Recommendations and are subject to effective systems for monitoring and ensuring their compliance with those requirements. Banks should also refer to the Basle CDD paper (section 2.2.4) which provides specific guidance concerning situations where an account holding institution may rely on a customer that is a professional financial intermediary to perform the customer due diligence on his or its own customers (i.e. the beneficial owners of the bank account). Where relevant, the CDD paper could also provide guidance in relation to similar accounts held by other types of financial institutions.*

*Simplified CDD or reduced measures could also be acceptable for various types of products or transactions such as (examples only):*

- *Life Insurance Policies where the annual premium is no more than USD/€1000 or a single premium of no more than USD/€2500.*

- *Insurance policies for pension schemes if there is no surrender clause and the policy cannot be used as collateral.*

- A pension, superannuation or similar scheme that provides retirement benefits to employees, where contributions are made by way of deduction from wages and the scheme rules do not permit the assignment of a member's interest under the scheme.

Countries could also decide whether financial institutions could apply these simplified measures only to customers in its own jurisdiction or allow them to do for customers from any other jurisdiction that the original country is satisfied is in compliance with and has effectively implemented the FATF Recommendations.

Simplified CDD measures are not acceptable whenever there is suspicion of money laundering or terrorist financing of specific higher risk scenarios apply.

## Setting the Mechanism for Identification Evidence

Customer identification has become one of the most important aspects of an anti-money laundering strategy and the requirements can be complex. The obligations placed on financial institutions and non-financial sector businesses must therefore be capable of being met by a conscientious institution in a practical way. Where best practice can be applied, the objective should be to require identification of both name and address separately from official documentation or sources.

Different countries take varying approaches to the documentary evidence required. In countries which have a national identity card system, that card is specified in legislation and regulation as providing the basis for identification. In countries which do not have such a system, no one particular document is specified, and financial institutions must determine their own approach based upon available documentation and records; such institutions often gain a cumulative satisfaction of identity from various sources.

Many Commonwealth countries do not have a national identity card system, and in a number of countries the proportion of the population having formal photographic documentation confirming their identity may be as low as 5 per cent. It is therefore necessary to devise an approach that will ensure an adequate degree of customer identification, without denying access to the financial system to those who have no formal identification documents.

As part of their financial and economic reforms, some Commonwealth countries have sought to increase the proportion of the population subject to some form of official identification to combat electoral fraud and to improve the efficiency of tax collection. Where possible, other grounds for requiring identification – including tackling money laundering – should be taken into account in administering this process. Ideally this would extend to including a photograph on the identification document, but failing that, the signature of the person identified would be acceptable, assuming literacy on the part of those wishing to open accounts and undertake transactions. If financial institutions were allowed access to a register of names and addresses, this would also assist in confirming that customers presenting such identification were who they claimed to be.

Where no system of identification exists for the majority of the population, it may be appropriate for identification procedures to be concentrated where there is the greatest risk of money laundering. At the most basic level, this would be where the sums of money involved were large or involved hard currency, or where there was movement of money in and out of the jurisdiction.

By and large, those individuals with large quantities of money are more likely to have formal identification documents, such as passports or driving licences and have their address registered for official purposes. The same is likely to be true of those customers who handle foreign currency or make transactions involving other countries.

For those countries where wide-scale identification is not possible, it might be reasonable to require identification from customers conducting transactions over a certain size, or who hold accounts that may exceed a certain limit. Identification should also be required for all foreign currency accounts and for all transactions over a certain amount involving the transmission of funds into or out of the country. However, such an approach is less satisfactory than one involving comprehensive customer identification and will not meet international standards.

Where international best practice cannot be met at the outset, it will be necessary for financial sector supervisors, other regulators and law enforcement agencies to monitor the effectiveness of the procedures and to introduce enhanced requirements as circumstances permit or the need arises.

## Identification of Legal Entities and Structures

A significant proportion of criminal money is laundered through the accounts and vehicles established on behalf of private companies or trusts and identification procedures that require transparency of ownership and control are therefore extremely important. FATF Recommendations 33 and 34 state that:

33. *Countries should take measures to prevent the unlawful use of legal persons by money launderers. Counties should ensure that there is adequate, accurate and timely information on the beneficial ownership and control of legal persons that can be obtained or accessed in a timely fashion by competent authorities. In particular, countries that have legal persons that are able to issue bearer shares should take appropriate measures to ensure that they are not misused for money laundering and be able to demonstrate the adequacy of those measures. Countries could consider measures to facilitate access to beneficial ownership and control information to financial institutions undertaking the requirements set out in Recommendation 5.*

34. *Countries should take measures to prevent the unlawful use of legal arrangements by money launderers. In particular, countries should ensure that there is adequate, accurate and timely information on express trusts, including information on the settlor, trustee and beneficiaries, that can be obtained or accessed in a timely fashion by competent*

*authorities. Countries could consider measures to facilitate access to beneficial owner-ship and control information to financial institutions undertaking the requirements set out in Recommendation 5.*

Private companies are particularly vulnerable to being used for money laundering and a full range of identification measures should be required, including the personal identification of principal shareholders and directors.

Companies listed on a regulated stock exchange are less vulnerable to being used for money laundering because of their public accountability. Identification of principal shareholders and directors is not therefore necessary. However, such companies are not immune from many of the underlying criminal offences such as fraud, bribery or corruption. Individual employees may also use the company's name as a smokescreen to mask illegal activity. Consequently, in the case of listed companies, confirmation that the company's representative has the authority to act is a vital requirement.

## Identifying Underlying Beneficial Ownership

The ultimate objective of any anti-money laundering strategy must be to take the profit out of crime. To be able to confiscate the proceeds of any crime, the beneficial owner must be identified and located. In many cases, the true owners of criminal funds will attempt to conceal their identities behind nominees or other people acting on their behalf.

Seeking the identity of the underlying beneficial owner can be of particular importance in the case of an offshore trust or an international business company where ownership is masked by nominee directors.

## Non-Face-to-Face Customers

Financial institutions and other businesses are increasingly asked to open accounts and enter into other relationships on behalf of customers who do not present themselves for personal interview. This has always been a frequent event in the case of non-resident customers, but the practice has increased significantly with the development of postal and electronic banking and internet services. In recognition of this, FATF Recommendation 8 states that:

> *Financial Institutions should pay special attention to any money laundering threats that may arise from new or developing technologies that might favour anonymity, and take measures, if needed, to prevent their use in money laundering schemes. In particular, financial institutions should have policies and procedures in place to address any specific risks associated with non-face to face business relationships or transactions.*

The Basle Committee has considered this issue in some depth and the Basle CDD paper contains the following advice for banking supervisors which again is wholly relevant to other business sectors:

*A typical example of a non-face to face customer is one who wishes to conduct electronic banking via the Internet or similar technology. Electronic banking currently incorporates a wide array of products and services delivered over telecommunications networks. The impersonal and borderless nature of electronic banking combined with the speed of the transaction inevitably creates difficulty in customer identification and verification. As a basic policy, supervisors expect that banks should proactively assess various risks posed by emerging technologies and design customer identification procedures with due regard to such risks.*

*Even though the same documentation can be provided by face to face and non-face to face customers, there is a greater difficulty in matching the customer with the documentation in the case of non-face to face customers. With telephone and electronic banking, the verification problem is made even more difficult.*

*In accepting business from non-face to face customers:*

- *banks should apply equally effective customer identification procedures for non face to face customers as for those available for interview; and*

- *there must be specific and adequate measures to mitigate the higher risk.*

*Examples of measures to mitigate risk include:*

- *certification of documents presented;*

- *requisition of additional documents to complement those which are required for face to face customers;*

- *independent contact with the customer by the bank;*

- *third party introduction, e.g. by an introducer subject to the criteria established in paragraph 36 (and in FATF Recommendation 9); or*

- *requiring the first payment to be carried out through an account in the customer's name with another bank subject to similar customer due diligence standards.*

As stated in section 6.7.2, Commonwealth countries should ensure that they mitigate the risk posed by new technologies by ensuring that those institutions offering electronic and internet services are subject to the same regulation supervision and compliance monitoring requirements as those institutions that offer their services by traditional means.

## Reliance on Introducers and Third Parties to Obtain Identification Evidence

The performance of identification procedures can be time consuming and there is a natural desire to limit any inconvenience for new customers. In some countries it has therefore become customary for financial institutions to rely on the procedures undertaken by introducers or other third parties when business is being referred. FATF recognises this practice in Recommendation 9 as follows:

> Countries may permit financial institutions to rely on intermediaries or other third parties to perform elements (a)–(c) of the CDD process or to introduce business, provided that the criteria set out below are met. Where such reliance is permitted, the ultimate responsibility for customer identification and verification remains with the financial institution relying on the third party.
>
> The criteria that should be met are as follows:
>
> a) A financial institution relying upon a third party should immediately obtain the necessary information concerning elements (a)–(c) of the CDD process. Financial institutions should take adequate steps to satisfy themselves that copies of identification data and other relevant documentation relating to the CDD requirements will be made available from the third party upon request without delay.
>
> b) The financial institution should satisfy itself that the third party is regulated and supervised for, and has measures in place to comply with CDD requirements in line with Recommendations 5 and 10.
>
> It is left to each country to determine in which countries the third party that meets the conditions can be based, having regard to information available on countries that do not or do not adequately apply the FATF Recommendations.

Financial institutions and other businesses should be reminded that relying on due diligence conducted by an introducer, however reputable, does not in any way remove the ultimate responsibility of the recipient financial institution to know its customers and their business. In particular, financial institutions and other businesses should not rely on introducers that are subject to weaker standards than those governing their own 'know your customer' procedures or that are unwilling to share copies of due diligence documentation.

## Identifying Existing Customers

While the customer identification process applies naturally at the start of a relationship, financial institutions and other relevant businesses that are already well established when customer due diligence requirements are imposed will have many well established customers on their books. Existing customers can also create money laundering or terrorist financing risks. The Basle Committee 2001 CDD paper for banks contains the following statement which is equally relevant to other financial institutions and non-financial businesses:

> To ensure that records remain up to date and relevant there is a need for banks to undertake reviews of existing records. An appropriate time to do so is when a transaction of significance takes place, when customer documentation standards change substantially or when

*there is a material change in the way that the account is operated. However, if a bank becomes aware at any time that it lacks sufficient information about an existing customer, it should take steps to ensure that all relevant information is obtained as quickly as possible.*

Some jurisdictions, both within and outside FATF, have imposed a complete customer review on financial sector firms to be undertaken within a set time scale to ensure that sufficient information exists on all customers both existing and new. Other jurisdictions have adopted the 'risk and trigger' based approach suggested by the Basle Committee.

## Applying Additional Due Diligence to Higher Risk Situations

International standards need to be supplemented and/or strengthened by additional measures tailored to the risks within the financial and business systems of a particular jurisdiction and to the risks within particular institutions. Enhanced due diligence is required in relation to the higher risk bank accounts, for example private banking services offered to high net worth customers. In particular, the risks associated with politically exposed persons and correspondent banking relationships should be acknowledged.

## Politically Exposed Persons

Business relationships with individuals holding important government or public positions and with persons or companies clearly related to them may expose a financial institution or other business to significant reputational and/or legal risks.

Corruption by some government leaders and public sector officials (often referred to as 'politically exposed persons' (PEPS)) inevitably involves serious crime such as theft or fraud and has become of increasing global concern. The scale of illegal wealth acquired by corrupt leaders and officials, particularly in jurisdictions where corruption within government and society is endemic, often contracts starkly with the relative poverty of that county and/or its people. The proceeds of such corruption are often transferred to other jurisdictions and concealed through private companies, trusts or foundations, or under the names of relatives or close associates.

In view of the high profile of such cases, and the international impact, financial institutions and other professional firms that handle the proceeds of corruption will often face a major reputational risk and in some cases criminal charges can arise. FATF Recommendation 6 covers this in the following way:

*Financial institutions should, in relation to politically exposed persons, in addition to performing normal due diligence measures:*

*a) Have appropriate risk management schemes to determine whether the customer is a politically exposed person.*

*b) Obtain senior management approval for establishing business relationships with such customers.*

c) Take reasonable measures to establish the source of wealth and source of funds.

c) Conduct enhanced ongoing monitoring of the business relationship.

## Correspondent Banking and Similar Relationships

Correspondent banking, i.e. the provision of banking services by one bank ('the correspondent bank') to another bank ('the respondent bank') is an important feature in many Commonwealth countries, enabling banks to conduct business and services that they do not offer directly. However, if banks fail to apply an appropriate level of due diligence to such accounts, they expose themselves to a range of risks and may find themselves holding and/or transmitting money linked to corruption, fraud or other illegal activity. FATF Recommendation 7 states that:

*Financial institutions should, in relation to cross border correspondent banking and other similar relationships, in addition to performing normal due diligence measures:*

a) *Gather sufficient information about a respondent institution to understand fully the nature of the respondent's business and to determine from publicly available information the reputation of the institution and the quality of supervision, including whether it has been subject to a money laundering or terrorist financing investigation or regulatory action.*

b) *Assess the respondent institution's anti-money laundering and terrorist financing controls.*

c) *Obtain approval from senior management before establishing new correspondent relationships.*

d) *Document the respective responsibilities for each institution.*

e) *With respect to 'payable-through accounts', be satisfied that the respondent bank has verified the identity of and performed on going due diligence on the customers having direct access to accounts of the correspondent and that it is able to provide relevant customer identification data upon request to the correspondent bank.*

(Identification and 'know your customer' procedures are dealt with in more detail in Chapter 11.)

### 8.4.4 Establishing the Requirements for Recognition and Reporting of Suspicions

In order for a national strategy to succeed, it is essential that financial institutions, professional firms and other designated businesses (and within them individual members of staff) are required to report any knowledge of suspicion of money laundering in a timely fashion.

This requirement is covered by FATF Recommendation 13 as follows:

*If a financial institution suspects or has reasonable grounds to suspect that funds are the proceeds of criminal activity, or are related to terrorist financing it should be required, directly by law or regulation, to report promptly its suspicions to the financial intelligence unit (FIU).*

The inclusion by the FATF of the words 'or has reasonable grounds to suspect' introduces an objective test of suspicion rather than the previous subjective test. Because the objective test was not in the 1990 Recommendations and is still not a feature of the European Money Laundering Directives, few countries have, to date, included it within their anti-money laundering legislation and regulations. The UK is one exception and while the concept of 'reasonable grounds' to suspect has yet to be tested in the English courts, it is clear from the debates that took place at the time of its introduction that the UK Parliament intended reasonable grounds to include not only negligence, but also the concept of wilful blindness, i.e. the intentional and deliberate avoidance of the facts. This would include, for example, proceeding with a transaction or instruction while being deliberately blind to the potential illegal origin of the funds involved.

Where the objective test is enshrined in criminal law, for example within the offence of not reporting suspicions, it introduces one of the ways in which guilt is established. The offence might therefore be proved when there exist facts or circumstances from which an honest and reasonable person engaged in similar business would have inferred knowledge of formed the suspicion that another person was engaged in criminal activity or money laundering.

Recommendation 14 recognises that within the financial sector and the professions, customer confidentiality is a contractual requirement and those financial institutions and firms that are required to report their suspicions must be protected from being sued for breach of confidentiality by their customers. Equally, they must not be permitted to tip off their customers that a suspicion report has been made.

*Financial institutions, their directors, officers and employees should be:*

a) *Protected by legal provisions from criminal and civil liability for breach of any restriction on disclosure of information imposed by contract or by any legislative, regulatory or administrative provision, if they report their suspicions in good faith to the FIU, even if they did not know precisely what the underlying criminal activity was, and regardless of whether illegal activity actually occurred.*

b) *Prohibited by law from disclosing the fact that a suspicious transaction report (STR) or related information is being reported to the FIU.*

While the legal situation protects financial institutions and professional firms from civil action by clients or liability for breach of confidence, it does not by itself defend them against the reputational damage that might arise if a disclosure, made in good faith but not relating to actual criminal activity, were to become known to the customer to whom it related, and that customer made the fact public.

To ensure that reports of suspicions are handled swiftly and confidentially, there must be a clear chain of responsibility both within individual institutions and continuing up through the authorities, so that individuals and institutions know exactly where they should take their information. Legislation should acknowledge that once employees have reported internally, they have fully met their obligations.

These institutional arrangements should ensure that suspicions disclosures are only handled by a small number of people, all of whom are well trained and aware of the sensitive nature of this information. The money laundering reporting officer should be the key central figure in this reporting chain and the link with the financial investigators.

Regular and direct contact between institutions and the authorities responsible for handling suspicion disclosures should increase the confidence that financial institutions have in the handling of disclosures, and will also tend to help the investigators and central authorities to understand the concerns of financial institutions.

While money laundering legislation requires the co-operation of the financial sector in order to be effective, it is not the purpose of such legislation to turn private sector institutions and businesses into detectives. Businesses cannot be expected to invest a large amount of time and resources in investigating their own customers' affairs to ensure that they are not laundering money. On the other hand, it is important that financial institutions do not wilfully turn a blind eye to what their customers are doing. Striking the right balance is something that will come only with experience.

It is important that financial institutions and other businesses do not feel pressured into making 'defensive' disclosures (i.e. reporting to the authorities on the merest hint of an unusual transaction), but rather have the confidence to make the necessary commercial enquiries to confirm the substance of the suspicion. Legislation should permit the reporting of suspicions after the transaction has been undertaken, and should accept legitimate enquiries as reason for delay. (Recognition and reporting of suspicions is dealt with in more detail in Chapters 9 and 12.)

### 8.4.5 Record-keeping Requirements

Financial sector records provide a vital part of the audit trail in criminal investigations. The ability to track criminal money through different financial institutions across different jurisdictions and to identify the final structures, accounts or investments into which the criminal money is placed is essential, if the funds are to be confiscated.

FATF Recommendation 10 states that:

*Financial institutions should maintain, for at least five years, all necessary records on transactions, both domestic or international, to enable them to comply swiftly with information requests from competent authorities. Such records must be sufficient to permit reconstruc-*

tion of individual transactions (including the amounts and types of currency involved if any) so as to provide, if necessary, evidence for prosecution of criminal behaviour.

Financial institutions should keep records on identification, data obtained through the due diligence process (e.g. copies or records of official identification documents like passports, identity cards, driving licences or similar documents), accounts files and business correspondence for at least five years after the business relationship is ended.

The identification data and transaction records should be available to domestic competent authorities upon appropriate authority.

## Format of Records

The format in which records are to be retained needs to be determined in accordance with requirements for the admissibility of evidence in court proceedings. Timely retrieval of all records should also be required. (Record keeping is dealt with in more detail in Chapter 13.)

### 8.4.6 Awareness Raising and Training of Staff

Recommendation 15 states that financial institutions and other designated businesses should develop an ongoing employee training programme. Properly trained and motivated staff provide the first line of defence against money laundering. Financial institutions and other designated businesses should be required to take steps to ensure that all relevant staff are aware of their statutory obligations, their employers' procedures for guarding against money laundering, the need to recognise and report suspicions, and the risks of becoming involved with criminal money.

Commonwealth countries will need to determine whether relevant institutions should be required to test the competence of their staff and the extent to which the institutions themselves will be held responsible for the negligent or wilful acts of their employees. (Awareness raising and training is dealt with in more detail in Chapter 14.)

## 8.5 The Role of the Supervisory Authorities

FATF Recommendations 23 and 24 set out the requirements for Regulation and Supervision as follows:

23. Countries should ensure that financial institutions are subject to adequate regulation and supervision and are effectively implementing the FATF Recommendations. Competent authorities should take the necessary legal or regulatory measures to prevent criminals or their associates from holding or being the beneficial owner of a significant or controlling interest or holding a management function in a financial institution.

For financial institutions subject to the Core Principles, the regulatory and supervisory *measures that apply for prudential purposes and which are also relevant to money laundering, should apply in a similar manner for anti-money laundering and terrorist financing purposes.*

*Other financial institutions should be licensed or registered and appropriately regulated, and subject to supervision or oversight for anti-money laundering purposes, having regard to the risk of money laundering or terrorist financing in that sector. At a minimum, businesses providing a service of money or value transfers, or of money or currency changing should be licensed or registered, and subject to effective systems for monitoring and ensuring compliance with national requirements to combat money laundering and terrorist financing.*

24. *Designated non-financial businesses and professions should be subject to regulatory and supervisory measures as set out below.*

   a) *Casinos should be subject to a comprehensive regulatory and supervisory regime that ensures that they have effectively implemented the necessary anti-money laundering and terrorist financing measures. At a minimum:*

   - *casinos should be licensed;*

   - *competent authorities should take the necessary legal or regulatory measures to prevent criminals or their associates from holding or being the beneficial owner of a significant or controlling interest, holding a management function in, or being an operator of a casino.*

   - *competent authorities should ensure that casinos are effectively supervised for compliance with requirements to combat money laundering and terrorist financing*

   b) *Countries should ensure that the other categories of designated non-financial businesses and professions are subject to effective systems for monitoring and ensuring their compliance with requirements to combat money laundering and terrorist financing. This should be performed on a risk-sensitive basis. This may be performed by a government authority or by an appropriate self-regulatory organisation, provided that such an organisation can ensure that its members comply with their obligations to combat money laundering and terrorist financing.*

Whether or not a single body is given responsibility for ensuring compliance with all aspects of money laundering legislation, it is vital that a number of functions are carried out. These include:

- Ensuring financial institutions comply with the requirements;

- Providing a level playing field;

- Ensuring that financial institutions do not fall under the control of criminals or criminal organisations;

- Issuing guidance notes to assist financial institutions in meeting their obligations under the legislation;

- Providing training for the staff of financial institutions in appropriate systems to forestall, prevent and recognise money laundering.

### 8.5.1 Monitoring Compliance

While it is clearly the responsibility of each institution's management to comply with legislative and regulatory obligations, it is also necessary for the appropriate supervisory authority to ensure that institutions have in place systems that address the requirements of the FATF Recommendations, and the national legislation and regulations.

FATF Recommendation 29 states that:

*Supervisors should have adequate powers to monitor and ensure compliance by financial institutions with requirements to combat money laundering and terrorist financing, including the authority to conduct inspections. They should be authorised to compel production of any information from financial institutions that is relevant to monitoring such compliance and to impose adequate administrative sanctions for failure to comply with such requirements.*

The supervisory authority responsible for fulfilling this responsibility may need to inspect financial institutions' records, and, if necessary, interview their staff. Financial supervisors and central banks will often have such powers. Even where these authorities do not have primary responsibility for tackling money laundering within the financial sector, they may have an interest in any findings that a financial institution is not taking adequate steps to guard against money laundering, as this may give cause for concern in other contexts. In order to maximise the effectiveness of such inspections, while minimising the burdens imposed by the inspection process on financial institutions, where responsibilities lie with more than one agency it may be appropriate for one authority to conduct inspections on behalf of others. This will require close co-operation between all the agencies concerned.

### 8.5.2 Using Licensing to Prevent Criminal Control of Financial Institutions

It is generally assumed that financial institutions themselves recognise the desirability of co-operating with the authorities to ensure that they do not find themselves inadvertently doing business with criminals. In almost all cases this assumption is justified, and financial institutions genuinely do want to 'keep the crooks off the books'. However, this is not the case where financial institutions have been set up by, or subsequently fall under the control of, criminals or criminal organisations.

A financial institution that knowingly launders criminal proceeds, and then conceals this behaviour from the authorities, poses a severe threat to the entire financial sector, and offers criminal organisations the best prospect of accessing the sector without detection. Unsurprisingly, this has tempted criminal organisations in some countries to make active efforts to acquire control of financial institutions which, in itself, can lead to banking crises in the centres concerned.

It is essential that financial regulators and other authorities responsible for combating money laundering take steps to ensure that criminal organisations cannot take control of, or set up, banks or other financial institutions. The key to this is to ensure that applicants for licences to run financial institutions are adequately scrutinised to ensure that they are 'fit and proper' to conduct the business that they propose and that legitimate financial services business is actually conducted. Indeed, countries could consider imposing an ongoing fit and proper test to be applied to all directors and controlling interests in financial institutions. The existence of brass plate banks and/or banks whose capital is issued in the form of bearer shares will offer prime opportunities for the criminal money launderer.

## 8.6 Establishing Partnership and Commitment

As stated above, an effective anti-money laundering strategy requires a partnership approach. This must extend to a partnership between the supervisory authorities and the relevant institutions and businesses. The legislators and regulators cannot provide an effective system without the goodwill and active co-operation of the companies and businesses covered. Lack of consultation with the private sector can often result in requirements that are unworkable and are therefore ignored. The supervisory authorities should be easily approachable and accessible to deal with the problems that will arise and be prepared to bridge the gap between the relevant institutions and businesses and law enforcement agencies. .

FATF Recommendation 25 recognises the need for communication between the various parties stating that:

> The competent authorities should establish guidelines, and provide feedback which will assist financial institutions and designated non-financial businesses and professions in applying national measures to combat money laundering and terrorist financing, and in particular, in detecting and reporting suspicious transactions.

Information and guidance about money laundering prevention and compliance should be clearly written and freely available so that institutions are not thwarted in their attempts to tackle the problem and comply with legislation. The expectations of the supervisory authorities and law enforcement agencies should be clearly communicated to all concerned to ensure that a level playing field across the financial, professional and business sector is maintained.

The provision of financial sector guidance notes and training packages can help to establish a level playing field, thereby ensuring that all institutions are basing their strategies on a standardised approach and that the problems are put in context.

### 8.6.1 Providing Guidance Notes

It has been the experience of financial institutions in many countries where money laundering legislation has been introduced that compliance with the legislation is made easier by the provision of officially approved guidance notes. In some countries, such guidance notes may have been developed by appropriate government agencies/supervisors, while in others the task has been allotted to industry bodies.

Whoever is responsible, it is important that such guidance is:

- Accurate, reflecting the legal provisions in such a way that financial institutions can trust the guidance;

- Comprehensible, so that it is easy to use; and

- Kept up-to-date, so that it reflects any amendments to legislation, practical experience or changes in the market place.

For these reasons it is desirable for the drafting of guidance notes to involve not only the regulatory and law enforcement agencies responsible for supervising and operating the legislation, but also the financial institutions, professions and designated businesses themselves.

The guidance notes can provide a succinct explanation of the institutions' obligations under the legislation, and should set out good practice in complying with the law in a more detailed way than is possible in the text of the legislation. They should also give examples of what might be considered suspicious transactions, and what elements might be appropriate for inclusion in staff training programmes.

Compliance with the guidance notes should not be mandatory. They are for guidance, not cast in tablets of stone, and every financial institution should exercise judgement about how they can best meet their responsibilities. However, compliance with the guidance notes should be capable of providing an institution with a safe harbour in the event that their procedures are questioned by a supervisor or court, and any variations on them should require justification. Guidance notes can also provide a means of reacting quickly to changes in circumstances and market developments in a way that provides flexibility without obstructing desirable financial sector developments.

Part III provides additional guidance on financial sector procedures from which each jurisdiction can develop its own guidance notes.

### 8.6.2 Education and Training

While guidance notes form an invaluable adjunct to money laundering legislation, they work best when they are combined with relevant training for the staff of financial institutions. While it is appropriate for financial institutions to train their own staff, it is vital that those officers who are responsible for making suspicion disclosures, and therefore liaise with the supervisory authorities, receive sufficient training in their specific responsibilities. Such training is best provided in close association with the agencies responsible for the operation of the legislation.

Anti-money laundering training should cover a range of topics, in particular:

- The requirements placed on financial institutions under the legislation, including the duties to identify customers, keep records and train staff in the appropriate systems, as well as reporting suspicions;

- Recognising transactions which might relate to money laundering, and determining to what extent suspicions that cannot be validated might be filtered out and not passed on to the authorities;

- Understanding the sort of information that would be of value to the authorities, the extent to which follow-up information might be valuable, and what level of feedback might be expected in response to disclosures.

In some Commonwealth countries, the provision of training has been arranged in association with the financial sector trade associations, who have been able to devise appropriate manuals and materials for training staff at all levels within financial institutions. This approach has helped to develop mutual understanding between the authorities and the trade associations, which has allowed the effectiveness of the legislation to be monitored informally, and possible improvements to it to be identified at an early stage.

### 8.6.3 *Political Commitment and Resources*

Regardless of the adequacy of legislation, or the requirements placed on the financial, professional and business sectors any country's anti-money laundering strategy will fail if the competent authorities are not sufficiently resourced or committed. FATF Recommendations 30–32 cover this in the following terms:

30. *Countries should provide their competent authorities involved in combating money laundering and terrorist financing with adequate financial, human and technical resources. Countries should have in place processes to ensure that the staff of those authorities are of high integrity.*

31. *Countries should ensure that policy-makers, the FIU, law enforcement and supervisors have effective mechanisms in place which enable them to co-operate, and where appropriate co-ordinate domestically with each other concerning the development and implementation of policies and activities to combat money laundering and terrorist financing.*

32. *Countries should ensure that their competent authorities can review the effectiveness of their systems to combat money laundering and terrorist financing systems by maintaining comprehensive statistics on matters relevant to the effectiveness and efficiency of such systems. This should include statistics on the STR received and disseminated; on money laundering and terrorist financing investigations, prosecutions and convictions, on property frozen, seized and confiscated; and on mutual legal assistance or other international requests for co-operation.*

# 9
# Processing Reports, Investigation, Prosecution and Confiscation

## 9.1 Establishing a Central Reporting Agency

The development of a centralised unit (i.e. a financial intelligence unit) for the collection, analysis and dissemination of suspicion reports and intelligence to the investigation agencies has come to be regarded as an essential component of the anti-money laundering system.

FATF Recommendations 26 and 27 state that:

26. *Countries should establish a FIU that serves as a national centre for the receiving (and, as permitted, requesting), analysis and dissemination of STR and other information regarding potential money laundering or terrorist financing. The FIU should have access, directly or indirectly, on a timely basis to the financial, administrative and law enforcement information that it requires to properly undertake its functions, including the analysis of STR.*

27. *Countries should ensure that designated law enforcement authorities have responsibility for money laundering and terrorist financing investigations. Countries are encouraged to support and develop, as far as possible, special investigative techniques suitable for the investigation of money laundering, such as controlled delivery, undercover operations and other relevant techniques. Countries are also encouraged to use other effective mechanisms such as the use of permanent or temporary groups specialised in asset investigation and co-operative investigations with appropriate competent authorities in other countries.*

### 9.1.1 Formation or Strengthening of Financial Intelligence Units

FIUs need to be tailored to the requirements of the country in question, taking into account the statutory reporting requirements that have been imposed on the financial sector. There is no one model that can be set; at the simplest level, an FIU may comprise one person and an assistant with one desktop computer and may exist solely to process suspicion reports from the financial institutions, passing them on to a Financial Investigation Unit. At the more comprehensive and complex level, an FIU might comprise a number of staff, utilising complex computer systems to collect, analyse and collate intelligence from several sources. The nature of the FIU will depend upon the extent of computerised records in the jurisdiction that can be accessed and the nature of the reporting requirements within the money laundering legislation. The larger, more sophisticated FIUs should network with the Egmont Group's International Secure Web System and enter the Statement of Purpose permitting the sharing of intelligence with other FIUs within and outside the region.

It is likely that some countries will be unable to provide the institutional support to establish an FIU independent from an existing structure. In such cases, it is recommended that the FIU be established as a part of a Financial Investigation Unit (see section 9.3.1 below)

The FIU, as a sub-unit of a Financial Investigation Unit, can function effectively if the functions and responsibilities remain separate and distinct. While this may not be the ideal structure for the two entities, in light of their different roles, it would provide the infrastructure support necessary to obtain, analyse, and use information and evidence relating to money laundering and other financial crimes.

## 9.2 Processing Reports

The use of a standardised format in the reporting of disclosures is valuable and should be followed wherever possible; such a standard form should be provided to all institutions and duplicated in guidance notes. Completed forms can then be sent by post (or in urgent cases by facsimile message) to the central reporting agency. In more technologically advanced countries, financial institutions submitting regular high volumes of disclosures could transmit the information directly onto the reporting agency's financial database by means of secure data transfer, thus removing the need for paper disclosures.

Sufficient information should be disclosed to indicate the nature of, and reason for, the suspicion to enable the investigating officer to obtain a court order if necessary. If a particular offence is suspected, this should be stated to enable the report to be passed to the correct agency for investigation with the minimum of delay.

The use of a standard form should not, however, prevent a financial institution from disclosing any other relevant information or relevant backing documents. Where the reporting institution has additional relevant evidence that could be made available, the nature of this evidence should be clearly indicated.

The receipt of a disclosure should be acknowledged by the central reporting agency, and, if applicable, written consent should be given to the reporting institution to continue with the transaction or to operate the customer's account. However, in exceptional circumstances, such as the imminent arrest of a customer and consequential restraint of assets, consent to continue operating the account might not be given. The reporting institution concerned should at all times be kept appraised of the situation. Consent that may be given to continue with a transaction or to operate the customer's account should not be seen as a directive; the financial institution should still be able to apply management judgement as to whether it wishes to do so or not.

## 9.3 Investigating Reports

The effective implementation of anti-money laundering initiatives and regulations by law enforcement officials in many countries has, to date, been impeded by unfamiliarity with money laundering techniques, a lack of expertise in the conduct of complex financial investigations and asset tracing, and shortage of material and personnel resources. More specifically, there is a widespread need for the training of investigators in such areas as money laundering methodologies, financial investigations, asset tracing, the operation of domestic and international financial institutions, the acquisition and development of evidence from domestic and foreign sources, and case preparation and presentation. The lack of such expertise has often affected all areas of law enforcement related to money laundering and the investigation and prosecution of the underlying predicate offence, and has resulted in many cases not being pursued by the police. Consequently, the view is now generally held that specialist Financial Investigation Units or combined Financial Intelligence/Financial Investigation Units are needed.

### 9.3.1 Formation or Strengthening of Financial Investigation Units

Financial Investigation Units are units of police (and in some countries customs) investigators brought together and trained to conduct financial investigations. Such investigations may be relatively simple, such as that required to support confiscation of the proceeds of a crime from a local criminal upon conviction where money laundering has not taken place. Other investigations will be far more complex and require the analysis of financial and computer-generated records. Financial investigations are frequently the only means of collecting the information necessary to support money laundering and asset forfeiture prosecutions. Successful implementation and use of trained Financial Investigation Units are dependant upon the commitment to adequately staff these units with personnel, provide the necessary training and management support and make available sufficient equipment and materials to achieve the unit's goals.

Financial Investigation Units need to work in co-ordination with FIUs, where they are organisationally separate, and have access to information and analysis obtained by the FIU.

## 9.4 Establishing Confidentiality and Controls

Following receipt from the Financial Intelligence Unit or other central agency, access to disclosure reports should be restricted to trained financial investigators. Discreet enquiries may need to be made to confirm the basis of the suspicion and supplementary information may need to be obtained from the reporting institution or other sources. However, the customer should never be approached unless criminal conduct is identified.

Arrangements for handling suspicion reports should ensure that:

- When suspicions are passed on to investigators, they are passed only to known contacts within investigating authorities, who are themselves aware of the sensitivity of the information that they receive and respect the need for confidentiality;

- All information that is not either relevant to ongoing investigations or might provide leads for future investigations is destroyed at the earliest possible opportunity;

- Financial institutions are kept informed of developments relating to disclosures that they have made as quickly and as fully as possible; and

- Procedures are adopted to prevent, so far as possible, the names of those making the reports getting into the hands of money launderers.

## 9.5 Obtaining Evidence for Use in Investigations

FATF Recommendation 28 states that:

> When conducting investigations of money laundering and underlying predicate offences, competent authorities should be able to obtain documents and information for use in those investigations, and in prosecutions and related actions. This should include powers to use compulsory measures for the production of records held by financial institutions and other persons, for the search of persons and premises, and for the seizure and obtaining of evidence.

Enquiries will be necessary by the investigating team for the purpose of obtaining evidence to support a prosecution or to support an application for an order to restrain, freeze or confiscate criminal assets.

Requests for information to be used in evidence should be made to financial institutions, professional firms and other businesses under relevant court orders, thereby ensuring that any initial intelligence contained in a suspicion report can be treated as confidential information and not disclosed to the defendant.

In the event of a prosecution, existence of the suspicion report and the source of the information should be protected, as far as the disclosure of evidence rules allow. Maintaining the integrity of the confidential relationship between the law enforcement agencies and the financial institutions is of paramount importance.

The partnership between law enforcement and the financial sector is a vital part of the overall prevention strategy, but it must be recognised that the partnership cannot be developed overnight. The strengths and weaknesses of each partner need to be recognised and compensated for by the other, and the respected skills complemented. The financial sector must recognise that financial investigators cannot be fully cognisant with all the intricacies of the financial markets and, in turn, law enforcement officers must not expect to treat financial sector staff as unpaid detectives to compensate for scarce resources.

## 9.6 Providing Feedback from the Investigating Agency

The provision of feedback by the investigating authorities to the financial institution by whom suspicions are reported is an important element of any reporting system. The provision of general feedback to the financial sector on the volume and quality of disclosures and on the levels of successful investigations arising from the disclosures should be provided on a regular basis by the reporting agency.

This feedback is a vital part of the education process and is necessary if suspicion is to be removed from a possibly innocent customer. If a significant number of disclosures are being made that cannot lead to more than superficial investigation, then the reporting institutions need to be informed and advised as to how the situation can be improved.

The FATF has drawn up best practice guidelines on providing feedback to reporting institutions; these can be accessed through the FATF website (*www.fatf-gafi.org*).

## 9.7 Compilation of Statistics and Trends

The effectiveness of money laundering legislation can best be maintained by ongoing assessment of its impact. Not only will governments wish to know what impact the legislation is having, but financial institutions will also benefit from feedback about the disclosures that they make, in aggregate as well as on a case by case basis.

Such assessment might usefully take a number of forms:

- Statistical information detailing the number of disclosures made, the percentage which have been of value and the classes of institution that made the disclosures;

- Information on convictions obtained and assets confiscated, both domestically and as a result of international co-operation;

- Regular appraisals of the costs of the anti-money laundering regime to government and to the financial sector;

- Trends in laundering, both domestic and international.

Responsibility for analysis and feedback is best placed with the central reporting agency. The information should be provided regularly to the appropriate government department, to supervisors and to the financial sector institutions.

## 9.8 Powers to Trace, Freeze and Confiscate the Proceeds of Crime

Most crime is motivated by profit. The pursuit and recovery of the proceeds of crime can make a significant contribution to crime reduction and the creation of a safe and just society. Confiscating the proceeds of crime can:

- Send out the message that crime does not pay;

- Prevent criminals from funding further criminality;

- Underpin confidence in a fair and effective criminal justice system and show that no-one is above the law;

- Remove the influence of negative role models from communities;

- Deter people from crime by reducing the anticipated returns;

- Decrease the risk of instability in the financial markets.

Criminal asset confiscation also has the potential to be a cost-effective law enforcement intervention. A number of jurisdictions have demonstrated that effective confiscation policies can generate significant revenue flows that reduce the net costs to the criminal justice system.

For criminal assets to be removed, they must first be located and the beneficial owner identified. An asset confiscation programme will only work if accompanied by sound financial sector customer identification systems and a financial investigation capability to follow complicated money trails. The pursuit of criminal assets can also help to build a deeper understanding of criminal networks, improve detection rates generally and assist in linking individuals apparently unconnected with crimes to the underlying predicate offences from which the proceeds were generated.

### 9.8.1 Exchange of Information

The laundering process for criminally generated funds will cross many national boundaries. Mutual assistance and exchange of information between jurisdictions is therefore essential if the proceeds of crime are to be traced and confiscated.

FATF Recommendation 40 states that:

*Countries should ensure that their competent authorities provide the widest possible range of international co-operation to their foreign counterparts. There should be clear and effective gateways to facilitate the prompt and constructive exchange directly between counterparts, either spontaneously or upon request, of information relating to both money laundering and the underlying predicate offences. Exchanges should be permitted without unduly restrictive conditions. In particular:*

*a) Competent authorities should not refuse a request for assistance on the sole ground that the request is also considered to involve fiscal matters.*

*b) Countries should not invoke laws that require financial institutions to maintain secrecy or confidentiality as a ground for refusing to provide co-operation.*

*c) Competent authorities should be able to conduct inquiries; and where possible, investigations on behalf of foreign counterparts.*

*Where the ability to obtain information sought by a foreign competent authority is not within the mandate of its counterpart, countries are also encouraged to permit a prompt and constructive exchange of information with non-counterparts. Co-operation with foreign authorities other than counterparts could occur directly or indirectly. When uncertain about the appropriate avenue to follow, competent authorities should first contact their foreign counterparts for assistance.*

*Countries should establish controls and safeguards to ensure that information exchanged by competent authorities is used only in an authorised manner consistent with their obligations concerning privacy and data protection".*

When the competent authorities in any Commonwealth member state have information that is officially requested by another jurisdiction, measures should be taken to ensure that the information is exchanged promptly whenever possible. Restrictions on the exchange of information should be linked to the following circumstances:

- The requesting authority should perform similar functions to the authority to which the request is addressed;

- The purpose and scope of information to be used should be expounded by the requesting authority and the information transmitted should be treated according to the scope of the request;

- The requesting authority should be subject to the same obligation of professional or official secrecy as the authority to which the request is addressed;

- The exchange of information should be reciprocal.

### 9.8.2 Mutual Legal Assistance and Extradition

The focus of mutual legal assistance and extradition is covered in FATF Recommendations 36–39 as follows:

36. *Countries should rapidly, constructively and effectively provide the widest possible range of mutual legal assistance in relation to money laundering and terrorist financing investigations, prosecutions, and related proceedings. In particular, countries should:*

    a) *Not prohibit of place unreasonable or unduly restrictive conditions on the provision of mutual legal assistance.*

    b *Ensure that they have clear and efficient processes for the execution of mutual legal assistance requests.*

    c) *Not refuse to execute a request for mutual legal assistance on the sole ground that the offence is also considered to involve fiscal matters.*

*d)* Not refuse to execute a request for mutual legal assistance on the grounds that laws require financial institutions to maintain secrecy or confidentiality.

*Countries should ensure that the powers of their competent authorities required under Recommendation 28 are also available for use in response to requests for mutual legal assistance, and if consistent with their domestic framework, in response to direct requests from foreign judicial or law enforcement authorities to domestic counterparts.*

*To avoid conflicts of jurisdiction, consideration should be given to devising and applying mechanisms for determining the best venue for prosecution of defendants in the interests of justice in cases that are subject to prosecution in more than one country.*

37. Countries should, to the greatest extent possible, render mutual legal assistance notwithstanding the absence of dual criminality.

*Where dual criminality is required for mutual legal assistance or extradition, that requirement should be deemed to be satisfied regardless of whether both countries place the offence within the same category or denominate the offence by the same terminology, provided that both countries criminalise the conduct underlying the offence.*

38. There should be authority to take expeditious action in response to requests by foreign countries to identify, freeze, seize and confiscate property laundered, proceeds from money laundering or predicate offences, instrumentalities used in or intended for use in the commission of these offences or property of corresponding value. There should also be arrangements for co-ordinating seizure and confiscation proceedings, which may include the sharing of confiscated assets.

39. Countries should recognise money laundering as an extraditable offence. Each country should either extradite its own nationals, or where a country does not do so solely on the grounds of nationality, that country should, at the request of the country seeking extradition, submit the case without undue delay to its competent authorities for the purpose of prosecution of the offences set forth in the request. Those authorities should take their decision and conduct their proceedings in the same manner as in the case of any other offence of a serious nature under the domestic law of that country. The countries concerned should co-operate with each other, in particular on procedural and evidentiary aspects, to ensure the efficiency of such prosecutions.

*Subject to their legal frameworks, countries may consider simplifying extradition by allowing direct transmission of extradition requests between appropriate ministries, extraditing persons based only on warrants of arrests or judgements and/or introducing a simplified extradition of consenting persons who waive formal extradition proceedings.*

FATF has firmly stated that mutual legal assistance should be granted as promptly and completely as possible if formally requested. Laws or regulations prohibiting international exchange of information between judicial authorities (notably specific reservations formulated to the anti-money laundering provisions of mutual legal assistance treaties or provisions by countries that have signed a multilateral agreement), or placing highly restrictive conditions on the exchange of information will be considered to be detrimental. Obvious unwillingness to respond constructively to mutual legal assistance requests (e.g. failure to take the appropriate measures in due course or long delays in responding) will also be considered by the FATF to be a detrimental practice.

### 9.8.3 Commonwealth Secretariat Guide to National Procedures

The Commonwealth Secretariat provides a *Guide* to member countries practices and procedures relating to mutual assistance in criminal matters. The *Guide* provides details of the department or agency to whom requests for assistance should be directed within each member country.

# PART III

# Financial and Professional Sector Procedures

# 10

# Internal Controls, Policies and Procedures

## 10.1 Duty to Establish Policies and Procedures

No financial institution or professional sector firm is immune from the risk of being used to launder the proceeds of crime. The reputational risk from becoming involved with criminal money can be fatal for any financial institution or professional firm, regardless of whether a criminal prosecution is brought against the business. All relevant institutions and firms should therefore be vigilant in guarding against their involvement or misuse for money laundering activities

Financial institutions and professional firms should establish clear responsibilities and accountabilities to ensure that policies, procedures and controls are introduced and maintained which deter criminals from using their facilities for money laundering. Business relationships should not be entered into or funds accepted where there is reasonable cause to believe that the assets or funds concerned have been acquired illegally or represent the proceeds of criminal activity. In addition to complying with the law, such a policy makes good business sense and will help to guard against fraud and bad debts.

In line with the interpretative note to FATF Recommendation 15, relevant businesses should consider appointing a money laundering compliance officer at managerial level to undertake this role (which may in any case be a legal requirement). This role may be combined with that of the money laundering reporting officer (see section 10.3).

FATF Recommendation 15 states that:

*Financial institutions should develop programmes against money laundering and terrorist financing. These programmes should include:*

a) *The development of internal policies, procedures and controls, including appropriate compliance management arrangements, and adequate screening procedures to ensure high standards when hiring employees;*

b) *A ongoing employee training programme;*

c) *A audit function to test the system.*

Recommendation 16 extends this requirement to lawyers and accountants when they are carrying out financial transactions for clients relating to:

- Buying and selling of real estate;

- Managing of client money, securities or other assets;

- Management of bank, savings or securities accounts;

- Organisation of contributions for the creation, operation or management of companies;

- Creation, operation or management of legal persons or arrangements, and buying and selling of business entities.

## 10.2 The Need to Tailor Policies and Procedures

Financial institutions should consider the money laundering risks posed by the products and services they offer, and devise their procedures with due regard to those risks. The highest risk generally relates to those products or services where third party funds can be freely received or where funds can be paid to, or received, from third parties without evidence of identity of the third party being taken. For example, some of the highest risk products are those offering money transfer facilities through cheque books, telegraphic transfers, deposits from third parties, cash withdrawals or other means. Bank current accounts naturally fall within this category because third party funds are continually received for credit to the account and it would be wholly impractical to identify all providers of such funds.

Some of the lowest risk products are those where funds can only be received from a named investor by way of payment from an account held in the investor's name and where the funds can only be returned to the named investor. No third party funding or payments are possible and therefore the beneficial owner of the funds deposited or invested is always the same. Insurance products and some deposit/savings accounts generally fall within this category.

The geographical location of a financial institution's customer base will also affect the money laundering risk analysis. Financial institutions that have a significant proportion of their customer base,i located in countries

- without equivalent anti-money laundering strategies for the financial sector; or

- where cash is the normal medium of exchange; or

- where there is a politically unstable regime with high levels of public or private sector corruption; or

- that are known to be drug producing or drug transit countries

will need to consider what additional due diligence procedures are necessary to manage the enhanced risks of money laundering. Additional monitoring should also be considered and appropriate measures put in place to manage the enhanced risk of money laundering in respect of funds received from such countries.

The FATF Recommendations also recognise that a risk-based approach is necessary in relation to business with countries that have insufficient anti-money laundering strategies.

FATF Recommendation 21 states that:

*Financial institutions should give special attention to business relations and transactions with persons, including companies and financial institutions, from countries which do not or insufficiently apply the FATF Recommendations. Whenever these transactions have no apparent economic or visible lawful purpose, their background and purpose should, as far as possible, be examined, the findings established in writing and be available to the competent authorities., Where such a country continues not to apply or insufficiently applies the FATF recommendations countries should be apply to apply appropriate countermeasures.*

## 10.3 Appointment of Money Laundering Reporting Officer

Financial institutions, professional firms and other designated businesses will find it helpful to establish a central point of contact with enforcement agencies in order to handle the reported suspicions of their staff regarding money laundering. This person, for the sake of simplicity, is referred to as the 'Money Laundering Reporting Officer' (again, this may be a legal requirement). Relevant businesses should:

- Introduce procedures for the prompt validation of suspicions and subsequent reporting to the central reporting agency;

- Provide the MLRO with the necessary access to systems and records to fulfil this requirement;

- Establish clear accountabilities for the design and delivery of necessary education and training programmes; and

- Establish close co-operation and liaison with the enforcement agencies.

The MLRO should normally be a person who is employed within the institution or firm as a member of senior management and the role may be combined with that of money laundering compliance officer (see section 10.1). Where there are business operations over several jurisdictions, a separate MLRO should be appointed within each jurisdiction.

(The role of the MLRO is discussed in Chapter 12.)

## 10.4 The Objectives of a Compliance Policy

Before drafting detailed procedures, it is beneficial for a financial institution, professional firm, or other relevant business to address the key policy issues which impact on compliance, and within which the detailed procedures will operate.

The objective of the policy is two-fold:

- To communicate the institution's intent to managers and staff internally; and

- To provide evidence to an external party (such as a supervisor) of the institution's intent to comply.

The policy should be endorsed at senior level and should include:

- A statement of intent to comply with the spirit of domestic legislation;

- An explanatory statement of requirements of compliance in overseas subsidiaries/branches, or how compliance requirements from an overseas parent will be reconciled with domestic legislation;

- A statement of intent to comply with domestic/overseas guidance notes issued by supervisors, regulators or representative bodies;

- An explanatory statement of acceptable criteria (if any) for accepting business from a customer whose identity cannot be verified in accordance with the letter of the law. If there is to be any discretion, it should be stated who may exercise it;

- An explanatory statement of criteria for continuing, accepting or declining business when suspicious. Again, if there is to be any discretion, it should be stated who may exercise it;

- Definitions of responsibilities, covering compliance, reporting, education and training and audit (see below);

- A statement of the institution's disciplinary attitude to an employee's willful non-compliance.

## 10.5 Compliance Monitoring and Auditing

A sound anti-money laundering compliance policy should be established at board and senior management level. Management need to be satisfied that the risk of their institution being used for money laundering has been minimised and that any requirements under money laundering regulations to maintain such procedures has been discharged.

To enable the Board to assess compliance by the financial institution with the national legislation and strategies, it is good practice to commission an annual report from the money laundering compliance officer/MLRO. An annual compliance report might cover the following:

- Any changes made or recommended in respect of new legislation, rules or industry guidance;

- Any compliance deficiencies that have been identified relating to current policies and procedures, and either the action taken or recommendations for change;

- A risk assessment of any new products and services and the compliance measures that have either been implemented or are recommended;

- The nature of the review taken out on jurisdictions placed on the FATF NCCT list, the results of that review and the measures taken to close out, monitor or block further business with that jurisdiction;

- The number of internal reports that have been received from each separate division, product area, subsidiary, etc.;

- The percentage of those reports that have been submitted to law enforcement;

- The number and nature of enquires or court orders received from law enforcement either arising out of the reports or otherwise;

- Any perceived deficiencies in the reporting procedures and any changes implemented or recommended;

- Information concerning which staff have received training during the period, the method of training, and any results or observations arising out of the training;

- Any additional information concerning communications to staff;

- Any recommendation concerning additional resource requirements to ensure effective compliance.

As good practice, internal audit or the external auditors should be asked to verify, on a regular basis, compliance with policies, procedures and controls relating to money laundering prevention.

## 10.6 Communication of Policies to Staff

The communication of an institution or firm's policies and procedures to prevent money laundering, and training in how to apply those procedures, underpins all other anti-money laundering strategies. Staff who are meeting with customers or handling transactions or instructions will either be a firm's strongest defence against money laundering or its weakest link. The means by which their obligations are communicated to them, and the effectiveness of the associated training, will determine the success of the institution's anti-money laundering strategy.

It is also important that the procedures and responsibilities for monitoring compliance with, and the effectiveness of, money laundering policies and procedures are clearly laid down by all financial institutions and communicated to management and staff.

As stated in section 10.2, the variety of products and services that may be offered by firms, and the nature and geographical location of the customer base, carry with them different money laundering risks and vulnerabilities. Institutions and firms will therefore need to determine their strategy and communicate to staff any types of business that will not be accepted, or the criteria to be used either for rejected transactions or for closing out a business relationship that has deemed to have become too high a risk.

The means of delivering information to staff are considered in Chapter 14

## 10.7 Group Policies

Many financial institutions or professional firms are branches or subsidiaries of a group with its head office in a different jurisdiction which may require adherence to a group policy in respect of money laundering procedures.

FATF Recommendation 22 states that:

*Financial institutions should ensure that the principles applicable to financial institutions mentioned above are also applied to branches and majority owned subsidiaries located abroad, especially in countries which do not or insufficiently apply the FATF Recommendations to the extent that local applicable laws and regulations permit. When local applicable laws and regulations prohibit this implementation, competent authorities in the country of the parent institution should be informed by the financial institutions that they cannot apply the FATF Recommendations.*

A group policy might require that all overseas branches and subsidiaries undertake identification and record-keeping procedures at least to the standards in the home country or, if standards in the host country are more rigorous, to those higher standards. When complying with a group policy, a financial institution should ensure that its own policies in respect of verification of identity and record keeping do not fall below those recognised in the host state.

Even where a group policy exists, the offences to which the money laundering legislation in the host country relates must be adhered to in accordance with local laws and procedures to ensure that any local confidentiality requirements are not breached. Suspicions of money laundering must therefore always be reported within the jurisdiction where the suspicion(s) arose and the records of the related transaction(s) are held.

# 11

# Establishing Customer Due Diligence Procedures

## 11.1 'Know Your Customer' – The Basis for Recognition and Reporting

Having sufficient information about a customer or a prospective customer, and making effective use of that information, underpins all other anti-money laundering procedures and is the most effective weapon against being used to launder the proceeds of crime. In addition to minimising the risk of being used for illicit activities, it provides protection against fraud, enables suspicious activities to be recognised and protects individual institutions from reputational and financial risks.

### 11.1.1 The Basic Requirements of 'Know Your Customer'

The first requirement of knowing your customer for money laundering purposes is to be satisfied that a prospective customer is who he or she claims to be.

The second requirement of knowing your customer is to ensure that when a business relationship is being established, the nature of the business that the customer expects to conduct is ascertained at the outset in order to show what might be expected as normal activity. This information should then be updated as appropriate and as opportunities arise.

In order to be able to judge whether a transaction is or is not suspicious, financial institutions need to have a clear understanding of the legitimate business of their customers.

## 11.2 The Duty to Verify Identity

FATF Recommendation 5 covers the duty to verify the identity of individuals and legal entities as follows:[11] It states that:

*Financial institutions should not keep anonymous accounts or accounts in obviously fictitious names.*

*Financial institutions should undertake customer due diligence measures, including identifying and verifying the identity of their customers, when:*

- *establishing business relations;*
- *carrying out occasional transactions: (i) above the applicable designated threshold; or (ii) that are wire transfers in the circumstances covered by the Interpretative Note to Special Recommendation VII;*

- *there is a suspicion of money laundering or terrorist financing; or*

- *the financial institution has doubts about the veracity or adequacy of previously obtained customer identification data.*

*The customer due diligence (CDD) measures to be taken are as follows:*

a) *Identifying the customer and verifying that customer's identity using reliable, independent source documents, data or information.*

b) *Identifying the beneficial owner, and taking reasonable measures to verify the identity of the beneficial owner such that the financial institution is satisfied that it knows who the beneficial owner is. For legal persons and arrangements this should include financial institutions taking reasonable measures to understand the ownership and control structure of the customer.*

c) *Obtaining information on the purpose and intended nature of the business relationship.*

d) *Conducting ongoing due diligence on the business relationship and scrutiny of transactions undertaken throughout the course of that relationship to ensure that the transactions being conducted are consistent with the institution's knowledge of the customer, their business and risk profile, including, where necessary, the source of funds.*

*Financial institutions should apply each of the CDD measures under (a) to (d) above, but may determine the extent of such measures on a risk sensitive basis depending on the type of customer, business relationship or transaction. The measures that are taken should be consistent with any guidelines issued by competent authorities. For higher risk categories, financial institutions should perform enhanced due diligence. In certain circumstances, where there are low risks, countries may decide that financial institutions can apply reduced or simplified measures.*

*Financial institutions should verify the identity of the customer and beneficial owner before or during the course of establishing a business relationship or conducting transactions for occasional customers. Countries may permit financial institutions to complete the verification as soon as reasonably practicable following the establishment of the relationship, where the money laundering risks are effectively managed and where this is essential not to interrupt the normal conduct of business.*

*Where the financial institution is unable to comply with paragraphs (a) to (c) above, it should not open the account, commence business relations or perform the transaction; or should terminate the business relationship; and should consider making a suspicious transactions report in relation to the customer.*

*These requirements should apply to all new customers, though financial institutions should also apply this Recommendation to existing customers on the basis of materiality and risk, and should conduct due diligence on such existing relationships at appropriate times.*

## 11.2.1 When Must Identity Be Verified?

Reference must be made to local legislation to determine when it is necessary to verify identity and what exemptions can be applied. For example, identity does not usually need to be verified where the immediate customer is itself a regulated financial institution that is subject to anti-money laundering regulations.

Once identification procedures have been satisfactorily completed, and the business relationship has been established, as long as regular contact is maintained and records concerning that customer are kept in accordance with local requirements, no further evidence of identity is needed when transactions are subsequently undertaken unless doubts have arisen about the accuracy or adequacy of the identification evidence that has been obtained previously.

When an existing customer closes one account and opens another, or enters into a new agreement to purchase products or services, there is no need to re-verify identity as long as regular contact has been maintained. However, the opportunity should be taken to obtain any missing or additional information concerning customers and to re-confirm the name, address and signature. This is particularly important if there has been no recent contact with the customer, e.g. within the past twelve months or when a previously dormant account is re-activated.

In such circumstances, details of the previous account and identification evidence obtained, or any introduction records, should be transferred to the new account records and retained for the relevant period.

## 11.2.2 Whose Identity Should Be Verified?

Identification evidence should be obtained for all prospective customers and any other person on whose behalf the customer is acting.

Identification evidence should therefore be obtained:

- for all principal parties and signatories to an account or a business relationship;

- the ultimate beneficial owner(s) of funds being invested or deposited.

In respect of *joint applicants*, identification evidence should be obtained for *all* account holders, not only the first named.

It is important that for private companies, i.e. those not quoted on a recognised stock exchange, identification evidence is obtained for the ultimate beneficial owner(s) of the company and those with principal control over the company's assets, e.g. principal directors. Firms should be alert to circumstances that might indicate a change in company structure or ownership and make enquiries accordingly.

In respect of trusts, identity should be verified for those providing funds, i.e. the settlor(s) and those who are authorised to invest or transfer funds, or to make decisions on behalf of the trust (i.e. trustees, protectors, managers, etc.).

Reasonable measures should be taken to obtain sufficient information to distinguish those cases in which a business relationship is commenced or a financial transaction is conducted with a person acting on behalf of others. If it is established that a customer is acting on behalf of another, the identity of both should be verified unless the intermediary is itself subject to equivalent anti-money laundering procedures.

There may be other cases in which a financial institution may regard a person as its customer although it may have no contractual relationship with him or her. For example, a mutual fund administrator will often regard the promoter or sponsor of the fund as his customer. In such cases, terms of business should determine who should be included in the category of customer, the extent to which identity of the underlying investors should be verified and by whom.

### 11.2.3 Timing of Identification Requirements

What constitutes an acceptable timespan for obtaining satisfactory evidence of identity will usually be determined in the light of all the circumstances. These will include the nature of the business, the geographical location of the parties and whether it is practical to obtain the evidence before commitments are entered into or money changes hands.

Therefore, identification evidence should be obtained as soon as reasonably practicable after a relevant financial institution has contact with a customer with a view to:

(a)  agreeing with the customer to carry out a transaction; or

(b)  reaching an understanding with the customer that future transactions will be carried out.

A financial institution may start processing the business or application immediately, provided that it:

- Promptly takes appropriate steps to obtain identification evidence; and

- Does not transfer or pay any money out to a third party until the identity requirements have been satisfied.

The Interpretative note to FATF Recommendation 5 advises that:

*Examples of the types of circumstances where it would be permissible for verification to be completed after the establishment of the business relationship, because it would be essential not to interrupt the normal conduct of business include:*

- *Non-face to face business.*

- *Securities transactions. In the securities industry, companies and intermediaries may be required to perform transactions very rapidly, according to the market conditions at the time the customer is contacting them, and the performance of the transaction may be required before verification of identity is completed.*

- *Life insurance business. In relation to life insurance business, countries may permit the identification and verification of the beneficiary under the policy to take place after having established the business relationship with the policyholder. However, in all such cases, identification and verification should occur at or before the time of payout or the time where the beneficiary intends to exercise vested rights under the policy.*

*Financial institutions will also need to adopt risk management procedures with respect of the conditions under which a customer may utilise the business relationship prior to verification. These procedures should include a set of measures such as a limitation of the number, types and/or amount of transactions that can be performed and the monitoring of large or complex transactions being carried out outside of expected norms for that type of relationship. Financial institutions should refer to the Basle CDD paper (section 2.2.6) for specific guidance on examples of risk management measures for non-face to face business.*

### 11.2.4  Failure to Complete the Due Diligence Requirements

If identification evidence is not received, the funds must be returned to the applicant. In these circumstances, funds must never be returned to a third party. No further funds should be accepted for investment or credit to the customer's account unless satisfactory identification evidence is received.

The failure by an applicant to provide satisfactory identification evidence without adequate explanation may in itself lead to a suspicion that the depositor or investor is engaged in money laundering. Returning the funds by way of a payment drawn on the financial institution could therefore assist in the laundering process. Where money laundering is suspected, financial institutions should therefore consider making a report to the relevant agency, based on the evidence in their possession, before the funds are returned to the applicant. However, care should be taken to avoid tipping off the prospective customer.

The interpretative note to FATF Recommendation 5 covers this issue in the following terms:

#### Customer Due Diligence and Tipping-off

1. *If, during the establishment or course of the customer relationship, or when conducting occasional transactions, a financial institution suspects that transactions relate to money laundering or terrorist financing, then the institution should:*

   a) *Normally seek to identify and verify the identity of the customer and the beneficial owner, whether permanent or occasional, and irrespective of any exemption or any designated threshold that might otherwise apply.*

   b) *Make a STR to the FIU in accordance with Recommendation 13.*

2. *Recommendation 14 prohibits financial institutions, their directors, officers and employees*

*from disclosing the fact that an STR or related information is being reported to the FIU. A risk exists that customers could be unintentionally tipped off when the financial institution is seeking to perform its customer due diligence (CDD) obligations in these circumstances. The customer's awareness of a possible STR or investigation could compromise future efforts to investigate the suspected money laundering or terrorist financing operation.*

3. *Therefore if financial institutions form a suspicion that transactions relate to money laundering or terrorist financing, they should take into account the risk of tipping-off when performing the customer due diligence process. If the institution reasonably believes that performing the CDD process will tip off the customer or potential customer, it may choose not to pursue that process, and should file an STR. Institutions should ensure that their employees are aware of and sensitive to these issues when conducting CDD.*

## 11.3 Establishing Identity

A financial institution should establish to its satisfaction that it is dealing with a real person or organisation (natural, corporate or legal), and obtain identification evidence sufficient to establish that the applicant is that person or organisation.

The requirement in all cases is to obtain satisfactory evidence that a person of the name of the applicant lives at the address given and that the applicant is that person. For companies it is necessary to be satisfied that the company has identifiable owners and that its representatives can be located at the address provided. **Because no single form of identification can be fully guaranteed as genuine, or representing correct identity, the identification process will need to be cumulative and no single source or document can be used to verify both name and permanent address.**

An individual's identity comprises, as a minimum, his/her name and all other names used; the address at which s/he can be located; date of birth; and nationality/country of residence. In the case of a legal entity,(corporate, business, etc.), identity comprises the registered name and/or trading name, registered address and the nature of the business activities.

Any subsequent changes to the customer's name and address of which the firm becomes aware should be recorded as part of the ongoing 'know your customer' process.

### 11.3.1 Identification Information for Natural Persons

As an extension to its publication *Customer Due Diligence for Banks*, the Basle Committee has issued a general guide to account opening and customer identification which goes into greater detail than the FATF Recommendations. For example, paragraph 10 lists the following information that the Committee believes banks should hold in respect of their personal customers:

- Legal name and other names use (such as maiden name);

- Correct permanent address (the full address should be obtained – a post office box number is not sufficient);

- Telephone number, fax number and e-mail address;

- Date and place of birth;

- Nationality;

- Occupation, public position held and/or name of employer;

- An official personal identification number of other unique identifier contained in an unexpired official document (e.g. passport, identification card, residence permit, social security records, driving licence) that bears a photograph of the customer;

- Type of account and nature of the banking relationship;

- Signature.

## 11.3.2 Procedures for Verifying the Identity of Natural Persons

How identity is verified must be decided according to what is available and appropriate within the individual country, and the nature of identification evidence that an individual can be expected to produce. The availability of a compulsory national identity card provides an easy solution, although the acceptability of this as a single source of verification must depend on the security of its issue and authentication. Generally, it is advisable to require two separate pieces of identification evidence, one for personal identity and one for address, in order to guard against impersonation fraud.

Depending on the available evidence, the requirements can be prescriptive or flexible. In the absence of a national identity card, it is important that genuine local customers are not prevented from having access to basic banking and financial services merely because they do have the preferred documentary evidence of identity and cannot be expected to do so.

For business conducted face-to-face, personal identity can best be checked against an official document, bearing a photograph of the applicant. As stated above, address verification should also be obtained from an official or secure document. The documents seen should always be originals or legally or officially certified copies.

Again, paragraphs 11 and 12 of the Basle Committee Guidance state the following possible requirement for banks:

*The bank should verify this information by at least of the following methods:*

- *confirming the date of birth from an official documents (e.g. birth certificate, passport, identity card, social security records);*

- *confirming the permanent address (e.g. utility bill, tax assessment, bank statement, a letter from a public authority);*

- *contacting the customer by telephone, by letter or by e-mail to confirm the information supplied after an account has been opened (e.g. a disconnected phone, returned mail or incorrect e-mail address should warrant further investigation);*

- *confirming the validity of the official documentation provided through certification by an authorised person (e.g. embassy official, notary public).*

*The examples quoted above are not the only possibilities. In particular jurisdictions there may be other documents of an equivalent nature which may be produced as satisfactory evidence of customers' identity.*

### 11.3.3 Identity Requirements for Corporate Customers

Because of the complexity of their organisations and structures, corporate and legal entities are the most likely vehicles for money laundering, especially those that are private companies fronted by a legitimate trading company. Care should be taken to verify the legal existence of the applicant (i.e. the company) and to ensure that any person purporting to act on behalf of the applicant is fully authorised. Enquiries should be made to confirm that the company exists for a legitimate trading or economic purpose and that it is not merely a 'brass plate company' where the controlling principals cannot be identified. A visit to the place of business may also be made useful to confirm the true nature of the business activities.

If changes to the company structure or ownership occur subsequently, or if suspicions are aroused by a change in the nature of the business transacted, or the profile of payments through a company account, further checks should be made to ascertain the reason for the changes.

For private companies, in addition to verifying the legal existence of the business, the principal requirement is to look behind the corporate entity to identify the principal owners and controllers, including those who control the company's assets. Where the owner is another corporate entity, trust or special purpose vehicle, the objective is to undertake reasonable measures to look behind that company or entity and to verify the identity of the principals. What constitutes control for this purpose will depend on the nature of a company and may rest in those who are mandated to manage funds, accounts or investments without requiring further authorisation and who would be in a position to override internal procedures and control mechanisms. For partnerships, each partner should be identified, including any immediate family members that have ownership control.

If changes to the company structure or ownership occur subsequently, or if suspicions are aroused by a change in the nature of the business transacted or the profile of payments through a company account, further checks should be made to ascertain the reason for the changes.

When signatories to the account change, care should be taken to ensure that the identity of at least two current signatories has been verified. In addition, it may be appropriate to make periodic enquiries to establish whether there have been any changes to directors/shareholders or to the original nature of the business/activity. Such changes could be significant in relation to potential money laundering activity, even though authorised signatories have not changed.

Particular care should be taken in cases of entities (whether companies, trusts or otherwise) which conduct no commercial operations in the country in which their registered office is located or when control is exercised through nominee or shell companies.

The Interpretative Note to FATF Recommendation 5 contains the following statement in relation to legal persons and other corporate vehicles and structures:

*When performing elements (a) and (b) of the CDD process in relation to legal persons or arrangements, financial institutions should:*

a) *Verify that any person purporting to act on behalf of the customer is so authorised, and identify that person.*

b) *Identify the customer and verify its identity – the types of measures that would be normally needed to satisfactorily perform this function would require obtaining proof of incorporation or similar evidence of the legal status of the legal person or arrangement, as well as information concerning the customer's name, the names of trustees, legal form, address, directors, and provisions regulating the power to bind the legal person or arrangement.*

c) *Identify the beneficial owners, including forming an understanding of the ownership and control structure, and take reasonable measures to verify the identity of such persons. The types of measures that would be normally needed to satisfactorily perform this function would require identifying the natural persons with a controlling interest and identifying the natural persons who comprise the mind and management of the legal person or arrangement. Where the customer or the owner of the controlling interest is a public company that is subject to regulatory disclosure requirements, it is not necessary to seek to identify and verify the identity of any shareholder of that company.*

The relevant information or data may be obtained from a public register, from the customer or from other reliable sources.

The Basle Guidance outlines the following information that banks should obtain in respect of any entity that it is not a natural person:

- Name of institution;

- Principal place of institution's business operations;

- Mailing address of institution;

- Contact telephone and fax numbers;

- Some form of official identification number, if available (e.g. tax identification number);

- The original or certified copy of the Certificate of Incorporation and Memorandum and Articles of Association;

- The resolution of the Board of Directors to open an account and identification of those who have authority to operate the account;

- Nature and purpose of business and its legitimacy.

The Guidance goes on to state that the information should be verified by at least one of the following methods:

- For established corporate entities – reviewing a copy of the latest report and accounts (audited, if available);

- Conducting an enquiry by a business information services, or an undertaking from a reputable and known firm of lawyers or accountants confirming the documents submitted;

- Undertaking a company search and/or other commercial enquiries to see that the institution has not been, or is not in the process of being, dissolved, struck off, wound up or terminated;

- Utilising an independent information verification process, such as by accessing public and private databases;

- Obtaining prior bank references;

- Visiting the corporate entity, where practical;

- Contacting the corporate entity by telephone, mail or e-mail.

The Guidance states that the bank should also take reasonable steps to verify the identity and reputation of any agent that opens an account on behalf of a corporate customer, if that agent is not an officer of the corporate customer.

### 11.3.4 Trusts

While there are many legitimate uses for trusts, both for personal and commercial use, trusts are popular vehicles for criminals wishing to avoid identification procedures and mask the origin of the criminal money they wish to launder. The particular characteristics of trusts that attract the genuine customer, and the anonymity and complexity of structures that they can provide, are also highly attractive to money launderers.

Particular care needs to be exercised when trusts, special purpose vehicles or international business companies connected to trusts are set up in offshore locations with strict bank secrecy or confidentiality rules. Those created in jurisdictions without adequate money laundering procedures in place will warrant additional enquiries.

The principal objective for money laundering prevention via trusts, nominees and fiduciaries is to verify the identity of the provider of funds, i.e. the settlor; those who have control over the funds, i.e. the trustees; and any controllers, protectors or managers who have the power to remove or influence the trustees. The nature and purpose of the trust and the source of funding should be ascertained and verified. Any beneficiaries who are able to exercise influence over the trustees should also be verified.

### 11.3.5 Non-Face-to-Face Verification

The rapid growth in e-commerce and internet financial services has added a new dimension to identification and 'know your customer'. Any mechanism which avoids face-to-face or personal contact between the firm and its customers provides additional opportunities for criminals.

Any financial institution offering postal or internet products and services should implement procedures to identify and authenticate the customer to the same standards as it would for face-to-face business and should ensure that there is sufficient communication to confirm address and personal identity.

Clearly, photographic evidence of identity is inappropriate where there is no intention to meet with the customer face-to-face. However, it is important that the procedures adopted to verify identity are at least as robust as those for face-to-face identification and that reasonable steps are taken to avoid single or multiple fictitious applications or identity fraud for the purpose of money laundering. A risk-based approach is recommended depending on the nature of the products or services offered.

As with face-to-face identification, the procedures to check identity must serve two purposes:

- They must ensure that a person bearing the name of the applicant exists and lives at the address provided; and

- They must ensure that the applicant is that person.

To guard against the dangers of postal intercept and fraud, prospective customers *should not* be asked to send personal identity documents, e.g. passport, identity card or driving licence, by post.

Financial institutions should consider regular monitoring of internet based business, particularly if additional 'know your business' information is not available. If a significant proportion of the business is operated electronically, computerised monitoring systems that are designed to recognise unusual transactions and related patterns of transactions may be necessary to assist in recognising suspicious transactions.

## 11.4 Introduced Business: Reliance Between Regulated Institutions

### 11.4.1 Who Can Be Relied upon and in What Circumstances?

While the responsibility to obtain satisfactory identification evidence rests with the financial institution that is entering into the relationship with the customer, local regulations may permit reliance to be placed on another regulated firm to undertake the identification procedures or to confirm identity.

FATF Recommendation 9 now addresses this issue and states that where countries permit financial institutions and other designated firms to rely on intermediaries or other third parties to verify identity or to introduce business the criteria that should be met are as follows:

a) *financial institution relying upon a third party should immediately obtain the necessary information concerning elements (a)–(c) of the CDD process. Financial institutions should take adequate steps to satisfy themselves that copies of identification data and other relevant documentation relating to the CDD requirements will be made available from the third party upon request without delay.*

b) *The financial institution should satisfy itself that the third party is regulated and supervised for, and has measures in place to comply with CDD requirements in line with Recommendations 5 and 10.*

*It is left to each country to determine in which countries the third party that meets the conditions can be based having regard to information available on countries that do not or do not adequately apply the FATF recommendations.*

The interpretative note to Recommendation 9 clarifies that the recommendation does not apply to outsourcing or agency arrangements nor to relationships accounts or transactions between financial institutions for their clients (i.e. where the intermediary institution is acting in an agency capacity.

As good practice, the following underlying principles should be applied to introduced business:

- 'Know your introducer' principles should be established in the same way as those for 'know your customer';

- The introducing institution or person must be regulated for banking or financial or professional services;

- The introducing firm or person must be covered by money laundering legislation and regulations to the standards set out in the FATF Recommendations;

- Verification of identity should be undertaken to standards at least applicable to those that the institution relying on the introduction would be required to make itself;

- Local legislation may require that a relevant introduction certification should be completed by the introducing institution or person in respect of each applicant for business.

### 11.4.2 Corporate Group Introductions

Where a customer is introduced by one part of a financial sector group to another, local legislation might permit that it is not necessary for identity to be re-verified or for the records to be duplicated provided that:

- The identity of the customer has been verified by the introducing parent company, branch, subsidiary or associate in line with international standards;

- A group introduction certificate is obtained and placed on the customer's file;

- Arrangements are put in place to ensure that underlying records of identity in respect of the introduced customer are retained for the necessary period.

### 11.4.3 Correspondent Relationships

Transactions conducted through correspondent relationships need to be managed taking a risk-based approach. 'Know your correspondent' procedures should be established to ascertain whether the correspondent bank or counter-party is itself regulated for money laundering prevention and, if so, whether the correspondent is required to verify the identity of their customer to standards at least equivalent to those applicable to the financial institution itself. Where this is not the case, additional due diligence may be required.

FATF Recommendation 7 states that:

*Financial institutions should, in relation to cross-border correspondent banking and other similar relationships, in addition to performing normal due diligence measures:*

a) *Gather sufficient information about a respondent institution to understand fully the nature of the respondent's business and to determine from publicly available information the reputation of the institution and the quality of supervision, including whether it has been subject to a money laundering or terrorist financing investigation or regulatory action.*

b) *Assess the respondent institution's anti-money laundering and terrorist financing controls.*

c) *Obtain approval from senior management before establishing new correspondent relationships.*

d) *Document the respective responsibilities of each institution.*

e) *With respect of "payable-through accounts", be satisfied that the respondent bank has verified the identity of and performed ongoing due diligence on the customers having direct access to accounts of the correspondent and that it is able to provide relevant customer identification data upon request to the correspondent bank.*

FATF Recommendation 18 goes on to state that:

*Financial institutions should refuse to enter into, or continue, a correspondent banking relationship with shell banks. Financial institutions should also guard against establishing relations with respondent foreign financial institutions that permit their accounts to be used by shell banks.*

Additional due diligence measures on correspondent relationships should also include obtaining the following information:

- The volume and nature of transactions flowing through correspondent accounts should be monitored against pre-determined levels and destinations, and any material variances should be checked.

- The identity of any principal customers generating a significant proportion of transactions through the correspondent accounts should be advised.

- Arrangements should be made to ensure that correspondents advise the financial institution of any local Exchange Control regulations and any restrictions on international transfers.

Financial institutions and professional firms should also note that US banks and other firms can be expected, from time to time, to examine their correspondent relationships to ensure that the risk of receiving criminal money through those relationships is minimised and that details of policies and procedures to guard against money laundering and terrorist financing will generally be sought from respondent banks. Any financial institution acting as a conduit for funds flowing from higher risk countries to the USA via correspondent relationships should ensure that the necessary due diligence has been completed and that the beneficial owner of the funds has been satisfactorily identified.

### 11.4.4 Politically Exposed Persons

Many developing countries lose significant amounts of public sector revenues or aid funds through public sector corruption. A large proportion of these embezzled funds is placed with financial institutions, usually in other jurisdictions. Financial institutions should, therefore, take additional care if they become aware that a customer has been appointed as a senior government official or to a ministerial position. The costs of becoming involved with the proceeds of corruption can be significant, particularly if ownership of the funds is disputed. For example, a constructive trust suit can arise when a financial institution handles the proceeds of grand corruption or where a government minister or senior public sector official is charged with diverting government funds or aid money.

Accounts that fall into this category should be regularly monitored by a senior account manager for transactions or series of transactions above a pre-determined limit. 'Know your customer' procedures can assist in recognising when there is no logical answer to newly acquired wealth or source of funds in these circumstances.

FATF Recommendation 6 addresses this issue in the following terms:

*Financial institutions should, in relation to politically exposed persons, in addition to performing normal due diligence measures:*

a) *Have appropriate risk management systems to determine whether the customer is a politically exposed person.*

b) *Obtain senior management approval for establishing business relationships with such customers*

c) *Take reasonable measures to establish the source of wealth and source of funds.*

d) *Conduct enhanced ongoing monitoring of the business relationship.*

'Politically exposed persons' will include senior political figures, their immediate family and close associates.

- **Senior political figure** is a senior figure in the executive, legislative, administrative, military or judicial branches of a government (elected or non-elected), a senior figure of a major political party, or a senior executive of a government owned corporation. It includes any corporate entity, partnership or trust relationship that has been established by, or for the benefit of, a senior political figure.

- **Immediate family** typically includes the person's parents, siblings, spouse, children, in-laws, grandparents and grandchildren where this can be ascertained.

- **Close associate** typically includes a person *who is widely and publicly known* to maintain a close relationship with the senior political figure and includes a person who is in a position to conduct substantial domestic and international financial transactions on his or her behalf.

The risks can be reduced by conducting detailed 'know your customer' procedures at the outset of a relationship and on an ongoing basis where firms know, suspect, or are advised, that the business relationship is with a senior political figure. Taking a risk-based approach, financial institutions and professional firms, should consider developing and maintaining the following enhanced scrutiny and monitoring practices to address this issue:

- Financial institutions and professional firms should assess which countries with which they do business are most vulnerable to corruption. One source of information is the Transparency International Corruption Perceptions Index (see *www.transparency.org*).

- Financial institutions and professional firms that do have business in countries which are vulnerable to corruption should establish who are the senior political figures in that country and should seek to determine, as far as is reasonably practicable, whether or not their clients have any connections with such individuals (e.g. immediate family or close associates). Such connections may also arise after the business relationship has been established.

- Institutions and firms should be most vigilant where their clients are involved in businesses that are most vulnerable to corruption such as, but not limited to, oil or arms sales.

Accounts that fall into this category should be regularly monitored by a senior account manager for transactions or series of transactions above a pre-determined limit. 'Know your customer' procedures can assist in recognising when there is no logical answer to newly acquired wealth or source of funds.

## 11.5 Knowing the Customer's Business

As stated in section 11.1, financial institutions need to have a clear understanding of the legitimate business activities of their customers. This will include the financial circumstances of a customer or any person on whose behalf the customer is acting and any significant features in the transactions to be undertaken on their behalf.

Information concerning the financial circumstances and the normal business activities of a customer should be kept up-to-date and any changes or additional information obtained should be recorded in the customer's file. Customer contracts and terms of business should require customers to advise of changes in their name, address or principal signatories. Significant or regular variations against the normal patterns and levels of activity should be subject to additional enquiries. Effective use of customer information should be made in assessing whether a transaction or instruction might be linked to the proceeds of crime. The origin and beneficial ownership of funds presented in payment or deposited by customers provide a vital part in the audit trail for tracing and confiscating the proceeds of crime. In addition, for higher risk customers and relationships, obtaining evidence of sources of income and/or wealth, i.e. the economic activity that created the funds for deposit or investment, will be required. This can be particularly important in a private banking, wealth management context or when dealing with customers categorised as politically exposed persons.

# 12

# Recognition and Reporting of Suspicions

FATF Recommendation 13 contains the basic requirement for reporting suspicions in the following terms:

> *If a financial institution suspects or has reasonable grounds to suspect that funds are the proceeds of a criminal activity or are related to terrorist financing, it should be required, directly by law or regulation, to report promptly its suspicions to the financial intelligence unit (FIU).*

Recommendation 16 specifically extends this requirement to lawyers and accountants as follows:

> *The requirements set out in Recommendation 13 apply to all designated non-financial businesses and professions, subject to the following qualifications:*
>
> *a) Lawyers, notaries, other independent legal professionals and accountants should be required to report suspicious transactions when, on behalf of or for a client, they engage in a financial transaction in relation to the activities described in Recommendation 12(d). Countries are strongly encouraged to extend the reporting requirement to the rest of the professional activities of accountants, including auditing.*

Recommendation 11 concerns an additional requirement relating to vigilance in respect of large and unusual transactions:

> *Financial institutions should pay special attention to all complex, unusual large transactions and all unusual patterns of transactions, which have no apparent economic or visible lawful purpose. The background and purpose of such transactions should, as far as possible, be examined, the findings established in writing, and be available to help competent authorities and auditors.*

Legislation in each particular country will determine whether financial institutions, professional firms and other relevant businesses are required to undertake compulsory transaction reporting (CTR), i.e. routine reporting of transactions above a specified financial threshold; or only to report knowledge or suspicion of money laundering (reporting of suspicions); or to do both.

Countries with CTR requirements already in place will also need to introduce the reporting of suspicions in line with the FATF recommendations.

## 12.1 Compulsory Transaction Reporting

The basis for compulsory transaction reporting is set out in Section 7.4. The reporting limits, the information to be provided and the types of financial institutions and business activities within the scope of the requirements will be laid down in the legislation. As with exchange control regulations, the system is mechanistic, strictly controlled and the penalties for breaching the requirements can be high.

## 12.2 The Obligation to Report Knowledge or Suspicion of Money Laundering

### 12.2.1 What is Meant by Knowledge?

Knowledge is now generally defined in legal statutes to be actual knowledge.

### 12.2.2 What is Meant by Suspicion?

Suspicion is personal and subjective and falls far short of proof based on firm evidence. Suspicion has been defined by the courts as being beyond mere speculation and based on some foundation, i.e.:

- *A degree of satisfaction not necessarily amounting to belief at least extending beyond speculation as to whether an event has occurred or not; and*

- *Although the creation of suspicion requires a lesser factual basis that the creation of a belief, it must nonetheless be built upon some foundation*

Because financial sector staff are not trained to be detectives, a person who believed that a transaction was suspicious should not be expected to know the exact nature of the criminal offence or that the particular funds were definitely those arising from the crime.

### 12.2.3 What is Meant by Reasonable Grounds to Suspect?

In addition to a criminal offence arising when actual knowledge or suspicion of money laundering is proved, FATF Recommendation 13 introduces the requirement to disclose information when reasonable grounds exist for knowing or suspecting that another is engaged in money laundering. This introduces an objective test for one of the ways in which proof of guilt may be established. This arises when there are proved to be facts or circumstances from which an honest and reasonable person engaged in a business in the regulated sector would have inferred knowledge or formed the suspicion that another was engaged in money laundering.

In order not to fall foul of the objective test, it is likely that staff within financial institutions and other designated businesses would need to be able to demonstrate, taking a risk-based approach, that they took all reasonable steps in the particular circumstances to know the customer and the rationale for the transaction or the instruction. However, it should be noted that reasonable grounds to suspect cannot be based on generalities or stereotypical images of certain groups or categories of people being more likely to be involved in criminal activity.

The type of situations giving rise to suspicion will depend on an institution's customer base and the range of products or services. As some products and services are more vulnerable to money laundering than others, a risk-based approach might be appropriate. Illustrations of the type of situation that might give rise to reasonable grounds for suspicion in certain circumstances are:

- Transactions which have no apparent purpose and which make no obvious economic sense;

- Where the transaction being requested by the client, without reasonable explanation, is out of the ordinary range of services normally requested or is outside the experience of the firm in relation to the particular customer;

- Where, without reasonable explanation, the size or pattern of transactions is out of line with any pattern that has previously emerged;

- Where the customer refuses to provide the information requested without reasonable explanation;

- Where a customer who has entered into a business relationship uses the relationship for a single transaction or for only a very short period of time;

- The extensive use of offshore accounts, companies or structures in circumstances where the customer's needs do not support such economic requirements;

- Unnecessary routing of funds through third party accounts;

- Unusual investment transactions without any discernable profitable motive.

## 12.3 'Know Your Customer': The Basis for Recognising Suspicions

As stated in Chapter 11, satisfactory 'know your customer' procedures, e.g. identification evidence and effective use of 'know your business' information provide the foundation for recognising unusual and suspicious transactions. **Where there is a business relationship, a suspicious transaction will often be one that is inconsistent with a customer's known legitimate activities or with the normal business for that type of account.** Therefore, the first key to recognition is knowing enough about the customer and the customer's normal expected activities to recognise when a transaction, or series of transactions, is abnormal.

Sufficient guidance must be given to staff to enable them to recognise suspicious transactions. However, the type of situations giving rise to suspicions will depend on an institution's customer base and range of services and products.

Questions that staff might be encouraged to consider when determining whether an established customer's transaction might be suspicious are:

- Is the size of the transaction consistent with the normal activities of the customer?

- Is the transaction rational in the context of the customer's business or personal activities?

- Has the pattern of transactions conducted by the customer changed?

- Where the transaction is international in nature, does the customer have any obvious reason for conducting business with the other country involved?

**Examples of what might constitute suspicious transactions are given in Appendix B.** These are not intended to be exhaustive and only provide examples of the most basic ways by which money may be laundered. However, identification of any of the types of transactions listed should prompt further investigation and be a catalyst towards making at least initial enquiries about the source of funds.

Financial institutions might also consider monitoring the types of transactions and circumstances that have given rise to suspicious transaction reports by staff, with a view to updating internal instructions and guidelines from time to time.

### 12.3.1 Monitoring Procedures to Assist a 'Know Your Customer' Approach

Ongoing monitoring of customer activity, either through manual procedures or computerised systems, is one of the most important aspects of effective 'know your customer' procedures. The type of monitoring procedures introduced will depend on a number of factors, including the size and nature of the business and the complexity and volume of the transactions or activity. Financial institutions and professional firms can only determine when they might have reasonable grounds to suspect money laundering if they have the means of assessing when a transaction or instruction falls outside their expectations or when it falls within one of the circumstances that should normally give rise to further enquiry, such as those illustrated in section 12.2.3 above.

The extent of 'know your customer' information necessary both at the outset and later, and the transaction monitoring that is required, will need to be assessed taking a risk-based approach. However, the information requested and updated must be reasonable in the circumstances and regard must be had to a customer's right to privacy.

Higher risk accounts and customer relationships will generally require more frequent or intensive monitoring. For higher risk situations, e.g. private bank accounts and wealth management relationships, the following should be considered:

- Institutions and firms should assess whether they have adequate procedures or management information systems in place to provide relationship managers and MLROs with timely information. The type of information that may be needed includes transactions made through a customer's account that are unusual, the nature of a customer's relationship with the firm and any readily identifiable connected accounts and relationships.

- The personal circumstances and sources of wealth and income for higher risk customers should be recorded, reviewed on a regular basis and, wherever possible, verified to check their legitimacy.

- Institutions and firms should seek to develop a clear policy, procedures and controls in respect of business relationships with customers who are known, suspected, or advised to be politically exposed person or with persons and companies that are clearly related or associated with them. As all PEPs may not be identified initially, and because existing customers may subsequently acquire PEP status, regular reviews for identifying PEP customers should be undertaken.

- Institutions and firms should consider reviewing the 'know your customer' information held on file and the activity for higher risk customers at least annually. Consideration should be given to centralising data in order to streamline the audit of higher risk customers.

## 12.4 Reporting Suspicions

Legislation will generally contain a provision for staff to report suspicions of money laundering to a money laundering reporting officer. Some financial institutions may choose to require that such unusual or suspicious transactions be drawn initially to the attention of supervisory management to ensure that there are no known facts that will negate the suspicion before further reporting to the MLRO or an appointed deputy.

All financial institutions, professional firms and designated businesses should ensure that:

- Each relevant employee knows the identity and responsibilities of the MLRO;

- Each relevant employee knows to which person he/she should report suspicions;

- There is a clear reporting chain under which those suspicions will be passed without delay to the MLRO;

- All internal reports reach the office of the MLRO, even if a supervisor or manager believes the suspicion is not valid.

It is normal under most money laundering legislation that once an employee has reported his/her suspicion to the 'appropriate person', he/she has fully satisfied their statutory obligation.

### 12.4.1 Internal Reporting Procedures

**Reporting lines** should be as short as possible, with the minimum number of people between the person with the suspicion and the MLRO. This ensures speed, confidentiality and accessibility to the MLRO. Once the reporting procedure has commenced, it is advisable for it to be followed through to the MLRO, even if the suspicion has been set aside by management within the reporting chain. In such cases the report should be annotated with the comments of the supervisor or manager giving the reasons that remove the suspicion. No person other than the MLRO, the deputy MLRO or the person nominated by the MLRO to consider internal reports should decide that a suspicion is without foundation and will not be reported to NCIS.

**Larger groups** may choose to appoint assistant MLROs within divisions or subsidiaries to enable the validity of the suspicion to be examined before being passed to a central MLRO. In such cases, the role of the assistant MLROs must be clearly specified and documented. All procedures should be documented in an appropriate manual and job descriptions should be drawn up.

**All suspicions reported** to the MLRO should be documented (in urgent cases this may follow an initial discussion by telephone). In some organisations it may be possible for the person with the suspicion to discuss it with the MLRO and for the report to be prepared jointly. In other organisations the initial report should be prepared and sent to the MLRO.

Reports from staff should include:

- The name of the reporting person, department or branch;

- Full details of the customer;

- As full a statement as possible of the information giving rise to suspicion;

- The date when the person with the suspicion first received the information and became suspicious; and

- The date of the report.

**The MLRO should acknowledge receipt** of the report and at the same time provide a reminder of the obligation to do nothing that might prejudice enquiries, i.e. 'tipping off'. All internal enquiries made in relation to the report, and the reason behind whether or not to submit the report to the authorities, should be documented. This information may be required to supplement the initial report or as evidence of good practice and best endeavours if, at some future date, there is an investigation and the suspicions are confirmed.

## 12.5 The Role of the Money Laundering Reporting Officer

The type of person appointed as MLRO will vary according to the size of the financial institution and the nature of its business, but he or she should be sufficiently senior to command the necessary authority. Larger institutions may choose to appoint a senior member of their compliance, internal audit or fraud departments. In small institutions, it may be appropriate to designate the chief executive or chief operating officer. When several subsidiaries operate closely together within a group, there is much to be said for appointing an overall group MLRO.

Legislation may impose on the MLRO a significant degree of responsibility. He/she is required to determine whether the information or other matters contained in the transaction report received give rise to a knowledge or suspicion that a customer is engaged in money laundering.

In making this judgement, he/she should consider all other relevant information available within the institution concerning the person or business to whom the initial report relates. This may include a review of other transaction patterns and volumes through the account or accounts in the same name, the length of the business relationship and referral to identification records held.

If after completing this review, he/she decides that the initial report gives rise to a knowledge or suspicion of money laundering, then he/she must disclose this information to the appropriate authority.

The MLRO will be expected to act honestly and reasonably and to make their determinations in good faith utilising all the information available. Providing that the MLRO or an authorised deputy does act in good faith in deciding not to pass on any suspicions report, there should be no liability for non-reporting if the judgement is later found to be wrong.

### 12.5.1 Formal and Documented Deliberations of the MLRO

If the suspicion raised is an 'open and shut case', the MLRO should report it immediately. In other cases the MLRO is required to evaluate the substance of the suspicion by way of confidential enquiry within the organisation. The MLRO is not required to undertake any enquiries with other organisations. The MLRO may request an appropriate person to make discrete enquiries of the customer, taking care to avoid any risk of tipping off.

Suspicion falls far short of proof based on firm evidence. It may, however, have substance in many ways, and may be based on the nature of the business being offered, an unusual transaction, etc.

The MLRO's enquiries must therefore be suited to the circumstances of the case. As a basis of approach, it is sensible for the MLRO to enquire into:

- Client identification and location;

- Type of business or pattern of business;

- Length of business relationship;

- Source and destination of funds; and

- Existence of earlier suspicions.

After making the enquiry, the MLRO must decide whether or not to make a report to the authorities.

After the enquiries have been undertaken, the decision and the reasoning behind it should be documented and retained securely. This information will be required either for the report to the authorities, or as evidence of good practice and best endeavour, if at some future date there is an investigation and the suspicions are confirmed.

Any documents called for by the MLRO as part of the enquiry should be listed and retained.

## 12.6 Reporting Suspicions to the Authorities

National legislation will determine the central reporting point within the various agencies. This is usually a financial intelligence unit within law enforcement.

If there is a standard report form, it should be used whenever possible. On all occasions when a report to the authorities has been made by telephone, it should be confirmed in writing.

The reporting institution should provide as much information as possible with regard to the suspicion, i.e. give the full story or as much as is known.

The information provided might usefully be structured to show:

- Information and suspicion initially reported to the MLRO;

- Enquiries undertaken by the MLRO; and

- The MLRO's reason for disclosing.

'One line' explanations of suspicion with reference to documents attached are not helpful; those receiving the reports may not be financial experts, and the documents themselves will often require interpretation.

### 12.6.1 Reporting Suspicions – The Tax Smokescreens

Initially, anti-money laundering legislation was confined to the proceeds of drug trafficking. The international move to 'all crimes anti-money laundering legislation' has changed the scope of crimes which are reported, although many countries do not include tax evasion within the scope.

Criminals soon learned that if they explained that an unusual or large cash transaction was being handled that way 'for tax reasons', financial sector staff asked no further questions. Consequently, the interpretative note to Recommendation 13, states:

*In implementing Recommendation 13, suspicious transactions should be reported by financial institutions regardless of whether they are also thought to involve tax matters. Countries should take into account that, in order to deter financial institutions from reporting a suspicious transaction, money launderers may seek to state inter alia that their transactions relate to tax matters.*

### 12.6.2 Secure Record Retention

All copies of reports and records should be retained and stored securely. The minimum requirement is lockable (and locked) filing cabinets with known key distribution.

It is suggested that the original of all internal reports should be filed upon receipt, with a copy for the MLRO's use. The MLRO's own 'suspicion evaluation record' should be treated similarly: the original should remain on file and any subsequent work should be done on a copy.

Records of suspicions raised internally but not disclosed should be retained for five years from the date of the transaction/suspicion.

Records of suspicions passed on to the reporting authority, but which the reporting authority have not advised are of interest, should be retained for a similar period.

Records of suspicions passed on to the reporting authority which are of interest should be retained until the authority has advised that they are no longer needed. If this causes any difficulties, the difficulties should be shared with the reporting authority or the investigating officer.

### 12.6.3 Protection of Staff Against Breach of Confidentiality

Normally financial sector staff would not divulge information concerning the accounts of transactions of their customers to third parties. Often banking secrecy legislation has rendered such action a criminal offence. The FATF has recognised this important issue and, as part of the national strategy FATF Recommendation 14 states that:

*Financial institutions, their directors, officers and employees should be:*

*a) Protected by legal provisions from criminal and civil liability for breach of any restriction on disclosure of information imposed by contract or by any legislative, regulatory or administrative provision, if they report their suspicions in good faith to the FIU, even if they did not know precisely what the underlying criminal activity way, and regardless of whether illegal activity actually occurred.*

## 12.7 Confidentiality of Disclosures – Tipping Off

One of the most important requirements of a suspicious transaction reporting regime is that reports made are treated in absolute confidence. It is essential that the customer, or prospective customer, should never become aware that a report has been made. One of the reasons for this is to guard against the risk of tipping off a customer that his/her account or transactions is/are under investigation. Tipping off is a criminal offence is many countries.

FATF Recommendation 14 b) states that:

*Financial institutions, their directors, officers and employees should be*

b) *prohibited by law from disclosing the fact that a suspicious transaction report (STR) or related information is being reported to the FIU.*

Internal confidentiality of reports is also important and, for this reason, the internal reporting chain should be kept as short as possible. The more people in the chain who are aware of a suspicious disclosure, the greater the chance of tipping off either deliberately or inadvertently.

In most countries, the confidentiality of disclosures will normally be honoured by law enforcement during their investigations. If the suspicion is proved to be valid, law enforcement will serve a court order on the financial institution to obtain the information required to enable a prosecution to be developed. It is the evidence that will usually be presented in court. However, this cannot be guaranteed if the original disclosure is considered to be essential to the case.

## 12.8  Liaising with the Investigating Agencies

The MLRO will normally be appointed as the central point of liaison with the authorities concerning disclosures and issues arising out of them.

In the event that the disclosure report is of immediate interest to the authorities, either because an investigation is already underway or an arrest is imminent, or because there is concern that the suspected finds may be paid away, the authorities may make a specific request concerning the account or the particular transaction. Permission to undertake the transaction or continue operating the account may in fact be required following a suspicious disclosure.

In the event that a financial institution wishes to close out an account or a relationship following one or more suspicion reports, the MLRO should liaise with the investigating agencies and agree what course of action should be taken, or what explanation can be given to the customer to avoid tipping off the customer that a report has been made.

# 13

# Retention of Records

## 13.1 General Principles and Objectives

FATF Recommendation 10 states that:[12]

> *Financial institutions should maintain, for at least five years, all necessary records on transactions, both domestic or international, to enable them to comply swiftly with information requests from competent authorities. Such records must be sufficient to permit reconstruction of individual transactions (including the accounts and types of currency involved if any) so as to provide, if necessary, evidence for prosecution of criminal behaviour.*

> *Financial institutions should keep records on the identification data obtained through the customer due diligence process, (e.g. copies or records of official identification documents like passports, identity cards, driving licenses or similar documents), account files and business correspondence for at least five years after the account is closed.*

> *The identification data and transaction records should be available to domestic competent authorities upon appropriate authority.*

When carrying out their investigations, enforcement agencies rely to a large extent on the integrity of documentation and information supplied by financial institutions. A financial institution should be able, within a reasonable time and if requested by the appropriate authorities, to demonstrate whether a particular person is its customer, or if they are the beneficial owner of assets deposited or invested, or if they have effected cash transactions requiring identification. In addition, the financial institution should be able to identify all the accounts, products and services from which the person identified is entitled to benefit.

The records prepared and maintained by any financial institution on its customer relationships and transactions should be such that:

- The requirements of legislation are fully met;

- Competent third parties will be able to judge reliably the institution's transactions and its observance of any policies and procedures;

- Any transactions effected via the institution can be reconstructed;

- All suspicion reports received internally, and those made externally, can be identified; and

- The institution can satisfy within a reasonable time any enquiries or orders from the appropriate authorities as to disclosure of information.

## 13.2 Identity Records

Records retained must:

- Indicate the nature of the evidence of identity obtained; and

- Comprise either a copy of the evidence or provide such information as would enable a copy of it to be obtained or sufficient to enable details of identity to be re-obtained. Sometimes legislation demands that actual copies must always retained.

Records should indicate that the originals of identification documents have been seen. The records containing evidence of identity must be kept for the period specified in the national legislation after the relationship with the customer has ended. The date when the relationship with the customer has ended is not always clear. Experience indicates that it should be considered as the date of:

- The carrying out of a one-off transaction or the last in the series of transactions; or

- The ending of the business relationship, i.e. the closing of the account or accounts; or

- The commencement of proceedings to recover debts payable on insolvency.

Where formalities to end a business relationship have not been undertaken, but a period of five years has elapsed since the date when the last transaction was carried out, then the five-year retention period commences on the date of the completion of the last transaction.

## 13.3 Transaction Records

In the case of transactions undertaken on behalf of customers, the supporting evidence and records, consisting of the original documents or copies admissible in court proceedings, must be retained for the period specified in the legislation following the date on which the relevant transaction or series of transactions is completed. These will be records in support of entries in the accounts in whatever form they are used.

The investigating authorities need to be able to compile a satisfactory audit trail for suspected laundered money and to be able to establish a financial profile of any suspect account. For example, the following information may be sought as part of an investigation into money laundering:

- The beneficial owner of the account (for accounts where intermediaries are involved, the identification of beneficial owner may need to be by way of a chain of verification procedures undertaken through the intermediaries concerned);

- The volume of funds flowing through the account.

For selected transactions:

- The origin of the funds;

- The form in which the funds were offered or withdrawn, i.e. cash, cheques, etc.;

- The identity of the person undertaking the transaction;

- The destination of the funds; and

- The form of instruction and authority.

Internal procedures need to ensure that *all transactions* undertaken on behalf of that customer are recorded on the customer's account. For example, a customer's records should include all requests for wire transfer transactions where settlement is provided in cash rather than funds drawn from the customer's account or reinvested.

Where the records relate to ongoing investigations, they should be retained until it is confirmed by the relevant law enforcement agency that the case has been closed.

## 13.4 Records of Suspicion Reports

It is recommended that records of all suspicion reports received from staff and all external reports to the competent authorities should be retained for five years. Where the money laundering reporting officer has considered information concerning a suspicion, but has not made a report to the authorities, a record of that information should be retained together with the reasons why the report was not considered to be valid.

## 13.5 Format and Retrieval of Records

### 13.5.1 Format of Records

It is recognised that financial institutions will find it necessary to rationalise their hard copy filing requirements. Most will have standard procedures which seek to reduce the volume and density of records which have to be stored, while still complying with statutory requirements. Retention may therefore be by way of original documents, documents stored on microfiche, or computerised or electronic records, subject to their being in a format that is admissible as evidence in court proceedings.

However, the record retention requirements are the same regardless of the format in which they are kept, or whether the transaction was undertaken by paper or by electronic means.

Documents held centrally must be capable of distinguishing between the transactions relating to different customers and of identifying where the transaction took place and in what form.

### 13.5.2 Retrieval of Records

The overriding objective is for firms to be able to retrieve relevant information without undue delay. Court orders, granted to an investigating officer, will usually require that the information specified should be available within a specified number of days from the date of the service of the order.

When setting document retention policy, financial institutions must weigh the statutory requirements and the needs of the investigating authorities against normal commercial considerations.

Nevertheless, financial institutions should ensure that when original documents, which would normally have been destroyed, are required for investigation purposes, they check that the destruction policy has actually been adhered to before informing the law enforcement agencies that the documents are not available.

### 13.5.3 Records Relating to Ongoing Investigations

Where the records relate to ongoing investigations, they should be retained until it is confirmed by the relevant law enforcement agency that the case has been closed.

## 13.6 Group Record Retention Policy

Where documents verifying the identity of a customer are held in one part of a group, they may not need to be held in duplicate form in another. However, if the documents are held in another jurisdiction, they must, wherever possible (subject to local legislation), be freely available on request within the group or otherwise be available to the investigating agencies under due legal procedures and mutual assistance treaties. Access to group records should not be impeded by confidentiality or data protection restrictions.

Financial institutions should also take account of the scope of money laundering legislation in other countries and should ensure that group records kept in other countries are retained for the required period.

Particular care should be taken to retain or hand over the appropriate records when an introducing branch or subsidiary ceases to trade or have a business relationship with a customer while the relationship with other group members continues. Such arrangements also need to be made if a company holding relevant records becomes detached from the rest of the group.

## 13.7 Wire Transfer Transactions

Investigations of major money laundering cases over the last few years have shown that criminals make extensive use of electronic payment and message systems. The rapid movement of funds between accounts in different jurisdictions increases the complexity of investigations. In addition, investigations become even more difficult to pursue if the identity of the original ordering customer or the ultimate beneficiary is not clearly shown in an electronic payment message instruction.

### 13.7.1 The Introduction of International Standards to Combat Terrorism

At an extraordinary plenary on the Financing of Terrorism held in Washington DC on 29–30 October 2001, the Financial Action Task Force (expanded its mission beyond money laundering. During the plenary, the FATF agreed on and issued new international standards to combat terrorist financing, which it calls on all countries to adopt and implement. The agreement on the Special Recommendations commits members, inter alia, to strengthen customer identification measures in international and domestic wire transfers. FATF Special Recommendation VII states:

> Countries should take measures to require financial institutions, including money remitters, to include accurate and meaningful originator information (name, address and account number) on funds transfers and related messages that are sent, and the information should remain with the transfer or related message through the payment chain.

> Countries should take measures to ensure that financial institutions, including money remitters conduct enhanced scrutiny of and monitor for suspicious activity funds transfers which do not contain complete originator information (name, address and account number).

The FATF issued an Interpretative Note to Special Recommendation VII on 14 February 2003.

By November 2003, all banks worldwide will have migrated to SWIFT MT 103 message format which will incorporate designated fields to enable disclosure of the name, address and account number of the originator. The originator is defined as the account holder or, where there is no account, the person (natural or legal) that places the order with the financial services business to perform the wire transfer.

Until that date, banks worldwide will be building systems designed to populate these designated fields; the FATF recognises that there will need to be a sensible lead time in which to enable systems and procedures to be adopted, many of which will be developed at group level, which provide for compliance with FATF Recommendation VII: 'Wire Transfers' and its Interpretative Note. Time will also be required by all countries to consider and address any legal and customer security issues that may arise from implementation of FATF Recommendation VII. Consequently, many countries agreed to be in full compliance with Recommendation VII by January 2005.

### Scope

The term *wire transfer* refers to any transaction carried out on behalf of an originator (both natural and legal persons) through a financial services business by electronic means with a view to making an amount of money available to a beneficiary at another financial services business. The originator and beneficiary may be the same person.

The term is not intended to cover the following types of payments:

- Any transfer that flows from a transaction carried out using a credit or debit card so long as the credit or debit card number accompanies all transfers flowing from the transaction. However, when credit or debit cards are used as a payment system to effect a money transfer, they will be subject to the requirements for cross-border or domestic wire transfers, as appropriate.

- Transfers between financial institutions and settlements where both the originator person and the beneficiary person are financial services businesses acting on their own behalf.

## Role of Ordering Financial Services Businesses

From the date of implementation, the ordering financial services business must ensure that qualifying wire transfers contain complete originator information, as set out below.

### Cross-border wire transfers

Originator information accompanying cross-border wire transfers must always contain:

- the name of the originator, and where an account exists, the number of that account. In the absence of an account, a unique reference number must be included; and

- either the address of the originator, his/her national identity number, a customer identification number, or date and place of birth.

FATF Special Recommendation VII defines cross border transfer as any wire transfer where the originator and beneficiary are located in different jurisdictions.

### Domestic wire transfers

Information accompanying domestic wire transfers must also include originator information as required for cross-border transfers, unless full originator information can be made available to the beneficiary financial services business and the FIU by other means. In this latter case, financial institutions may include only the account number of a unique identifier provided that this number will permit the transaction to be traced back to the originator.

Where financial institutions choose to benefit from the concession permitted for domestic transfers, the ordering business should be required to make complete originator information available within three days of receiving the request either from the beneficiary financial services business or the FIU.

FATF Special Recommendation VII defines a domestic transfer as any wire transfer where the originator and beneficiary institutions are located in the same jurisdiction. The term therefore refers to any chain of wire transfers that takes place entirely within the borders of a single jurisdiction, even though the system used to affect the wire transfer may be located in another jurisdiction.

## Role of Intermediary and Beneficiary Financial Services Businesses

From the date of implementation, financial institutions processing an intermediary element of a chain of wire transfers will be required to ensure that all originator information remains with the transfer or related message through the payment chain.

Where technical limitations prevent the full originator information accompanying a cross-border wire transfer from remaining with a related domestic wire transfer (during the necessary time to adapt payment systems), a record must be kept for five years by the receiving intermediary financial institution of all the information received from the ordering financial institution and made available on request to the beneficiary financial institution and to the FIU.

From the date of implementation, beneficiary financial institutions should have effective risk-based procedures in place to identify wire transfers lacking complete originator information. The lack of complete originator information may be considered as a factor in assessing whether a wire transfer or related transactions are suspicious and, as appropriate, whether they are thus required to be reported to the FIU. In some cases, the beneficiary financial institution should consider restricting or even terminating its business relationship with financial institutions that fail to meet standards set in FATF Recommendation VII: Wire Transfers and its Interpretative Note.

### 13.7.2 Record Keeping

Records of electronic payments and messages must be treated in the same way as any other records in support of entries over an account and kept for a minimum of five years.

# 14

# Awareness Raising and Training

## 14.1 Communicating Information to Staff

The communication of policies and procedures to prevent money laundering, and training in how to apply those procedures, underpin all other anti-money laundering strategies. The effectiveness of any anti-money laundering strategy, must depend on the extent to which staff in relevant institutions and firms appreciate the serious nature of the background against which the anti-money laundering and counter-terrorism legislation and regulations have been issued.

All staff, whether they are handling relevant financial transactions or not, should normally be subject to criminal law relating to money laundering. Consequently, they should be informed that they can be personally liable for failure to report knowledge or suspicion of money laundering that is gained in the course of their business activities. All staff should also be advised that, as well as criminal sanctions, disciplinary proceedings may also arise if they become involved in laundering the proceeds of crime.

Although directors and senior managers may not be involved in the day-to-day procedures, it is important that they understand the statutory duties placed on them, their staff and the firm itself.

### 14.1.1 Awareness Raising

Financial institutions, professional firms and other relevant businesses should ensure that all relevant staff are aware of:

(a) Their responsibilities under the institution's arrangements for money laundering prevention including those for obtaining identification evidence, 'know your customer', and recognising and reporting knowledge or suspicion of money laundering;

(b) The identity and responsibilities of the MLRO;

(c) The law relating to money laundering; and

(d) The potential reputational risks of becoming involved in laundering the proceeds of crime;

The variety of products and services available through relevant institutions and firms, and the nature and geographical location of the customer base, carry with them different money laundering risks and vulnerabilities. Financial institutions, professional firms and relevant businesses will therefore need to determine their strategy and communicate to staff any types of business that will not be accepted or the criteria to be used either for rejected transactions or for closing out a business relationship that has deemed to have become too high a risk.

### 14.1.2 Delivery of Information to Staff

In order to satisfy the legal and regulatory requirements for training, the provision of information to staff should be documented and its receipt recorded.

There is no fixed approach to the means of delivery but the following alternatives might be considered:

- Insertion of relevant information into existing procedure manuals, recognising that because the information may be split over separate sections, a separate summary document covering the money laundering procedures might be necessary.

- The preparation of an *Anti-Money Laundering and Counter-Terrorism Handbook* for management and staff. This would provide in one discrete location all information concerning the legislation and the tailored policies and procedures of the firm relating to the requirements of the rules and regulations together with the procedures for opening accounts or acquiring new business.

- When there is a large number of staff who do not need to be informed of the full details of the firms polices and procedures, a simplified awareness raising booklet might be appropriate.

Larger institutions and firms may choose to deliver the information electronically, for example over the internal 'intranet'.

## 14.2 Training

FATF Recommendation 15 states that:

> *Financial institutions should develop programmes against money laundering and terrorist financing. These programmes should include an ongoing employee training programme.*

All staff should be trained to be familiar with their systems for the reporting of suspicious matters to, and the investigation of such suspicious matters by, the MLRO.

### 14.2.1 Managers/Staff

All employees, regardless of their level of seniority, who will be dealing with customers, should be made aware of the need to report suspicious transactions and of the structure of the institution's reporting system.

Training should be provided on recognising suspicious factors and transactions, and on the procedure to be followed when a transaction is deemed to be suspicious. In particular, it is important that 'front line' staff are aware of the institution's policy for dealing with non-regular customers, particularly in respect of large cash transactions, and of the need for extra vigilance in these cases.

Members of staff who handle account opening should, in addition, be made aware of the need to verify the customer's identity, and training should be given in identity verification procedures. Such staff should be taught that the offer of suspicious funds or the request to undertake a suspicious transaction may need to be reported whether or not the funds are accepted or the transaction carried out.

A higher level of training should be given to supervisory and managerial staff. This should include familiarity with relevant legislation, and the requirement for the retention of records. Refresher training should be provided at regular intervals for all staff to ensure that they do not forget their responsibilities.

### 14.2.2 Compliance/Reporting Officers

In-depth training concerning all aspects of legislation, financial sector regulation and internal policies will be required for the MLRO. In addition, the MLRO will require extensive initial and ongoing instruction on the validation and reporting of suspicious transactions and on the feedback arrangements.

### 14.2.3 Timing and Approach to Training

The timing for training should be tailored to the needs of the particular group of staff concerned. Staff who meet customers or handle customer transactions will need more frequent training than others. There could be a rolling programme of training under which training on different subjects could take place on different dates.

While there is no standard way to conduct staff training for money laundering purposes, the vital requirement is that staff training must be relevant to those being trained and the training messages should reflect good industry practice.

The precise approach will depend on the size and nature of the organisation and the available time and resources. Classroom training, videos and technology-based training programmes can all be used to good effect depending on the environment and the number of people to be trained.

## 14.3 Keeping Records of Training

Records kept in relation to training should include the dates on which training was given, the nature of the training and the names of staff who received the training. Financial institutions, professional firms and other relevant businesses might find it helpful to put in place a student management system that incorporates the ability to record the training undertaken and the competency achieved within the training programme.

# Appendix A

# Money Laundering Typologies

The following typologies have been drawn from the typologies reports published by the FATF during the period 1997–2003.

## Introduction

The techniques used by money launderers are many and varied; they evolve to match the volume of funds to be laundered and the legislative/regulatory environment of the 'market place'. The sophisticated money launderer is like water running downhill; both seek out the line of least resistance. Thus in a cash-based society that has lax legal and regulatory controls, little effort is needed to disguise the cash or its ownership; consequently the launderer will fund his/her lifestyle in cash or, where funds need to be transferred or surplus funds deposited or invested, the launderer will deal directly with the banks in order to abuse basic banking facilities.

Where cash is not the norm, and legal and regulatory controls are sound, greater effort will be required to disguise the source of criminal cash and other funds and also to disguise their beneficial ownership. In consequence, the launderer may seek to set up corporate structures and trusts (both onshore and offshore) and attempt to present an appearance of legitimate commercial or financial enterprise as a disguise. It is an added bonus if such structures can be set up in a jurisdiction that itself has lax legislation and regulation or strict confidentiality controls. Finally, it is important to recognise that the launderers' techniques will evolve and change in line with the development of banking and other financial sector products and services.

This 'dynamic' view of the launderers' techniques is confirmed by the regular typology exercises that have been carried out over several years by the FATF and in addition, more recently, by other international and regional bodies. The reports of such exercises are available both in hard copy and over the internet; they should be considered essential reading in order to keep up-to-date with emerging trends.

In broad terms, typologies/techniques tend to fall into a number of discrete groups:

## 1. Cash and Banking Services

Cash deposits, basic banking and money transmission services remain the core means of laundering criminal proceeds. The small-time launderer will seek the benefits of the basic savings, deposit and current accounts, and personal and mortgage type lending. The more wealthy launderer will, of course, seek the services of specialist banking facilities serving the needs of the 'high net worth' individual.

The typical mechanisms for using banking services are as follows:

## Deposit structuring/smurfing

This technique entails making numerous deposits of small amounts below a reporting threshold, usually to a large number of accounts. The money is then frequently transferred to another account, often in another country. This method is widely used, even in countries which do not require cash transactions above certain thresholds to be reported. Countries to which these funds are transferred often find the funds being promptly removed as cash from the recipient accounts.

## Connected accounts

Identification requirements tend to deter criminals from opening accounts in false names. However, this is often replaced by the use of accounts held in the names of relatives, associates or other persons operating on behalf of the criminal. Other methods commonly used to hide the beneficial owner of the property include the use of shell companies, almost always incorporated in another jurisdiction, and lawyers. These techniques are often combined with many layers of transactions and the use of multiple accounts – thus making any attempts to follow the audit trail more difficult.

## Collection accounts

Collection accounts are a technique which is widely used by ethnic groups from Africa or Asia. Immigrants pay many small amounts into one account, and the money is then be sent abroad. Often the foreign account receives payments from a number of apparently unconnected accounts in the source country. While this payment method is certainly used for legitimate purposes by working immigrants and labourers who send money to their home country, this fact has been recognised by criminal groups who use this method to launder their illegitimate wealth.

## Payable through accounts

Payable through accounts are demand deposit accounts maintained at financial institutions by foreign banks or corporations. The foreign bank funnels all the deposits and cheques of its customers (usually individuals or businesses located outside the country) into one account that the foreign bank holds at the local bank. The foreign customers have signatory authority for the account as sub-account holders and can conduct normal international banking activities. Payable through accounts pose a challenge to 'know your customer' policies and suspicious activity reporting guidelines. It appears that many banks offering these types of accounts have been unable to verify or provide any information on many of the customers using these accounts, which poses significant money laundering threats.

## Cash deposits and telegraphic transfer

Large cash deposits are often made by drug traffickers or others who have smuggled criminal funds out of the country where the crime originated. Often the cash deposit is quickly followed by a telegraphic transfer to another jurisdiction, thus lowering the risk of seizure.

## Bank drafts, etc.

Bank drafts, money orders and cashiers' cheques, usually purchased for cash, are common instruments used for laundering purposes because they provide an instrument drawn on a respectable bank or other credit institution and break the money trail.

## Loan back arrangements

Loan back arrangements are often used in conjunction with cash smuggling. By this technique, the launderer usually transfers the illegal proceeds to another country, and then deposits the proceeds as a security or guarantee for a bank loan, which is then sent back to the original country. This method not only gives the laundered money the appearance of a genuine loan, but often provides tax advantages.

## Bureaux de change

Bureaux de change, exchange offices or casas de cambio offer a range of services which are attractive to criminals: (i) exchange services which can be used to buy or sell foreign currencies, as well as consolidating small denomination bank notes into larger ones; (ii) exchanging financial instruments such as travellers' cheques, euro cheques, money orders and personal cheques; and (iii) telegraphic transfer facilities. The criminal element continues to be attracted to bureaux de change because they are not as heavily regulated as traditional financial institutions or not regulated at all. Even when regulated, the bureaux often have inadequate education and internal control systems to guard against money laundering. This weakness is compounded by the fact that most of their customers are occasional, which makes it more difficult for them to 'know their customer', and thus makes them more vulnerable.

## Remittance services

Remittance services (sometimes referred to as giro houses) have also proved to be widely used for money laundering, since they are often subject to fewer regulatory requirements than institutions such as banks which offer an equivalent service. They are also popular with many ethnic groups as they charge a lower commission rate than banks for transferring money to another country, and have a long history of being used to transfer money between countries. They operate in a variety of ways, but most commonly the business receives cash which it transfers through the banking system to another account held by an associated company in the foreign jurisdiction, where the money can be made available to the ultimate recipient. Another technique commonly used by money remitters and currency exchanges is for the broker to make the funds available to the criminal organisation at the destination country in the local currency. The launderer/broker then sells the criminal funds to foreign businessmen desiring to make legitimate purchases of goods for export. This correspondent type operation resembles certain aspects of 'alternative remittance systems' (see Typology No. 2).

## Credit and Debit Cards

Structured cash payments for outstanding credit card balances are the most common use of credit cards for money laundering, often with relatively large sums as payments and in some instances by cash payments from third parties. A large number of identified scenarios involve the use of lost or stolen cards by third parties. Another method is to use cash advances from credit card accounts to purchase cashier's cheques or to wire funds to foreign destinations. On some occasions, cash advances are deposited into savings or current accounts. It is intended that this typology will be examined as part of a future FATF typologies exercise.

## 2. Alternative Remittance Systems/Value Transfer Systems

Alternative remittance systems (also called underground or parallel banking, informal money or value transfer systems) are almost always associated with ethnic groups from Africa, China or Asia, and commonly involve the transfer of value between countries, but outside the legitimate banking system. The 'broker', which may be set up as a financial institution such as a remittance company, or may be an ordinary shop selling goods, has an arrangement with a correspondent business in another country. The two businesses have customers that want funds in the other country, and after taking their commission the two brokers will match the amounts wanted by their customers and balance their books by transferring an amount between them for the time period, e.g. once a month. The details of the customers who will receive the funds, which are usually minimal, are faxed between the brokers, and the customers obtain their funds from the broker at the end of the transaction.

Often there is no physical movement of currency and there is a lack of formality with regard to verification and record-keeping. The normal *modus operandi* is that money transfer takes place by coded information passed through chitties, couriers, letters or fax, followed by a telephone confirmation. Almost any document which carries an identifiable number can be used for the purpose. Because there is no recognisable audit trail the launderer's chance of remaining undetected or avoiding confiscation is significantly increased.

The systems are referred to by different names depending upon the community being served, e.g. *Hawala* (an Urdu word meaning reference), *Hundi* (a Hindi word meaning trust), *Chiti* banking (referring to the way in which the system operates), *Chop Shop* banking (China) and *Poey Kuan* (Thailand).

There is evidence that terrorists use traditional methods of money transmission such as *Hawala* to move funds between jurisdictions. Such transactions often involve transfers from the UK through a third country, further obscuring the ultimate destination of the funds (see also *Typology No. 9 – Terrorist Financing*).

## 3. Investment Banking and the Securities Sector

At some stage of the laundering process, the successful launderer may wish to invest the proceeds. This investment may be by way of a stockbroker or a portfolio management service from an investment bank or directly with a securities house.

All types of securities, commodities, futures and options can be used as a means of money laundering. The wholesale market is attractive due to the ease and speed with which products can be purchased, sold, converted between currencies and transferred from one jurisdiction to another. A further attraction is the availability of bearer products and the large size of transaction. The high net worth individual or corporate launderer may not draw as much attention when washing large sums as they would in a more conventional banking operation.

### Cash-based transactions

The use of cash within the securities sector is relatively rare and many market operators are generally restricted or prohibited from accepting cash. Consequently, the use of the securities sector for laundering purposes is primarily part of the layering and integration stages. However, from time to time cash can be introduced through the sector, particularly where brokers break rules to accept cash, often for increased commissions. Another way within some countries is to accept cash for use in margin trading. In an effort to turn a quick profit, settlement within the margin trading market is often left until the last minute and cash then becomes the popular means of settlement.

### 'Pump and Dump' schemes

Market manipulation through the artificial inflation of a stock based on misleading information (a 'pump and dump' scheme) is also used to generate fraudulent proceeds. In addition, there have been cases where this type of securities fraud has been set up with the proceeds of other crimes and sometimes money laundering can be used to advance this fraud. In a typical 'pump and dump' scheme, individuals obtain large blocks of stock in a company before it is publicly traded or while it is dormant or not yet operational. A money launderer may use criminal proceeds to purchase these large blocks of stock. The shares are usually obtained at an extremely low price, and after the perpetrators have accumulated large stock holdings in the company, they may utilise unscrupulous brokers to promote the securities to their clients.

Misleading information is released into the public domain to promote the company and its business operations although the company will often have no legitimate operations. In order to create the appearance of market demand, the perpetrators of the securities fraud may divide transactions among several brokers and/or channel transactions through multiple jurisdictions. When the shares reach a peak price, the perpetrators sell off their shareholding and obtain a profit from the artificial inflation of the price. Eventually, the company is permitted to fail and the shares become worthless. At this point, two events have occurred, firstly the launderer, by selling his/her stock in the company has layered the illicit funds they originally invested; and, secondly, as a perpetrator of a securities fraud, they have generated additional illicit proceeds that require laundering.

## 4. Insurance and Personal Investment Products

Life policies and other personal investment products, and general insurance are attractive to the launderer. Life policies and personal investment products can often be purchased with cash, especially through small intermediaries. A useful ploy for the launderer is to purchase with cash followed by early cancellation or surrender of the policy.

In many jurisdictions life insurance polices are viewed as another form of investment, and it is this investment aspect that increases the vulnerabilities of the products. Because the insurance sector within many jurisdictions tends to view itself as lower risk for money laundering, the insurance broker may often prove to be one of the weakest links in an anti-money laundering strategy.

General insurance policies can also be an attractive laundering technique: putting an expensive asset on cover, paying a large premium by bank transfer, followed by early cancellation of cover asking for the refund remittance to be made to another bank in another country.

## 5. Internet and Electronic Financial Services

The number of financial institutions providing financial services on the internet is growing considerably with an increasing range of services becoming available (savings/deposit accounts, full cheque accounts, electronic fund transfers, stockbroking, insurance, etc.).

Delivery of financial services over the internet has been, in essence, a development from banking services and stockbroking services delivered by telephone. The challenge to the service provider and the attraction to the launderer is the absence of face-to-face contact.

Technology has provided the opportunity for more credit and financial institutions to offer electronic money. This may be by way of a card-based electronic purse. While the size/value of such 'purses' is restricted by regulatory requirement, the opportunity to purchase such electronic money for cash and then to use it to purchase assets, albeit modest, or obtain a refund by cheque, provides an opportunity for structured placement.

There are currently few case studies of money laundering through online financial services but whether this is due to a true lack of cases or the inability to detect such activity is not clear.

## Companies trading and other business activities

Companies, partnerships and sole trader businesses are used as a cover for money laundering. Cash-based businesses provide a cover for cash deposits into a bank account and the payment of suppliers, both domestically and internationally, provides a ready excuse for transfers of all sizes. Criminals may also pay an inflated price for stock in order to obtain control of a company and then use the company to inject the criminal proceeds along with the legitimate earnings, or use legitimately earned company profits to fund further criminal activity.

## International trade

International trade in goods and services can be used either as a cover for money laundering or as the laundering mechanism itself. Import/export activities and transactions are commonly used; a trader may pay a large sum of money (from the proceeds of illegal activity) for goods which are worthless and are subsequently thrown away or sold on cheaply. Alternatively, illegal proceeds can be used to buy high-value assets such as luxury cars, aeroplanes or boats which are then exported to narcotics-producing countries.

The launderer's priority is to make the transactions look normal. To achieve this the launderer will utilise all the normal trade finance services offered by the banks to legitimate import/export businesses.

## Shell corporations

The shell corporation is a tool which appears to be widely used in both the banking and non-banking sectors. Often purchased 'off the shelf' from lawyers, accountants or secretarial companies, it remains a convenient vehicle to launder money. It conceals the identity of the beneficial owner of the funds, the company records are often more difficult for law enforcement to access because they are offshore or held by professionals who claim secrecy, and the professionals who run the company act on instructions remotely and anonymously. These companies are used at the placement stage to receive deposits of cash which are then often sent to another country or at the integration stage to purchase real estate. They have also been the vehicle for the actual predicate offence of bankruptcy fraud on many occasions.

## 6. The Gold and Diamond Markets

### The gold market

Precious metals, and in particular, gold, offer the advantage of having a high intrinsic value in a relatively compact form. For some societies, gold carries an important cultural or religious significance that adds to the demand for the metal in certain regions of the world. The advantages that gold provides are also attractive to the money launderer, in particular its high intrinsic value, convertibility and potential anonymity in transfers. Most laundering schemes involving gold are linked to drugs trafficking, organised crime activities and illegal trade in merchandise and goods. The gold itself may be the proceeds of crime that needs to be laundered if, for example, it has been stolen or smuggled by creating a system of false invoicing.

Another more complex technique uses the gold or precious metal purchases and sales as a cover for the laundering operation.

### The diamond market

Illegal trade in diamonds has become an important factor in armed conflict in certain areas of the world, and terrorist groups are believed to be using diamonds from these regions to finance their activities. The ease with which diamonds can be hidden and transported, and the very high value per gram for some stones, make diamonds particularly vulnerable to illegal diversion from the legitimate channels for the exploitation and profit of criminals. As with gold, the simplest typology involving diamonds consists of direct purchase of the diamonds with criminal proceeds. Other common typologies using diamond trading activity include retail foreign exchange transactions, the purchase of gaming chips at casinos, forged or fraudulent invoicing, and the commingling of legitimate and illicit proceeds in the accounts of diamond trading companies.

It is believed that between 5 and 10 per cent of diamonds produced annually in one particular region are lost due to theft or pilferage which then form part of the illicit diamond market. Some of the illicit diamonds are known to provide income to purchase illicit arms and consequently these diamonds have been termed 'blood' diamonds.

## 7. Lawyers, Accountants and Other Intermediaries

Lawyers and accountants can become involved in money laundering through their role in setting up corporate and trust structures and when acting as directors or trustees. In addition, the client account can provide the launderer with a totally hidden route into a bank account. In some jurisdictions legislation may forbid the bank being provided with information relating to the identity of the client and the source of funds. Lawyers, accountants and other financial advisers can also be a useful means of laundering money through the sale of personal investment products (see *Typology No. 3*).

# 8. Terrorist Financing

There are two primary sources of financing for terrorist activities. The first method involves obtaining financial support from states or structures with large enough organisations to be able to collect and then make the funds available to the terrorist organisation. It is believed that this so-called state-sponsored terrorism has declined in recent years and has been superseded by backing from other sources.

The second method of raising funds for terrorist organisations is to obtain them directly from various 'revenue-generating' activities. These activities may include criminal acts; in this way they may appear similar to ordinary criminal organisations. Unlike such organisations, however, terrorist groups may also derive a portion of their revenues from legitimately-earned income. How much of a role legal monies play in the support of terrorism seems to vary according to the terrorist group and whether its source of funds is in the same geographic location as its terrorist acts.

## 'Legal' sources of terrorist financing

The ideological rationale for some terrorist movements means that individual terrorists or terrorist groups may sometimes rely on legally-generated sources of income. As mentioned above, this is a key difference between terrorist groups and traditional criminal organisations. Some of the specific fundraising methods include:

- Collection of membership dues and or subscriptions;

- Sale of publications;

- Speaking tours, cultural and social events;

- Door-to-door solicitation within the community;

- Appeals to wealthy members of the community; and

- Donations of a portion of their personal earnings.

## Donations

It is common practice within the Islamic community to donate a 'zakat', one tenth of one's income, to charity. There should be no assumption that such donations bear a relation to terrorist funding. However, donations continue to be a lucrative source of funds from private individuals, rogue states and the sale of publications. Such donations are often made on an irregular basis. There is also growing evidence that large donations made by wealthy individuals in the Middle East to charitable organisations that have connections with terrorist organisations are more associated with Mafia-style protection payments. The donation ensures that the donor's business interests remain untouched.

## 'Illegal' sources of terrorist financing

Criminality provides a much more consistent revenue stream. Terrorist organisations will choose activities that carry low risks and generate large returns. Major sources of income are:

- **Kidnap and extortion**

This form of money raising continues to be one of the most prolific and highly profitable. Monies are usually raised from within the community of which the terrorists are an integral part. Eventually extortion becomes a built-in cost of running a business within the community and the payment of ransom demands to free family members becomes an everyday occurrence.

- **Smuggling**

Smuggling across a border has become one of the most profitable ventures open to terrorist organisations. Smuggling requires a co-ordinated, organised structure, with a distribution network to sell the smuggled goods. It then offers high returns for low risks. Criminal partners will also benefit from their involvement, but there are considerable amounts made available for the terrorist organisation.

The profits can then be channelled via couriers to another jurisdiction. The money enters the banking system by the use of front companies or short-term shell companies that disappear after three months. Specialised bureaux de change may also be created, whose sole purpose is to facilitate the laundering of proceeds of the smuggling.

Another method of integrating the proceeds into the banking system has recently been detected. Monies are given by the smuggler to legitimate businesses who are not associated with the smuggling operation. These monies are then paid into the banking system as part of a company's normal turnover. Provided the individuals are not greedy, detection is extremely difficult. Monies are then sent via different financial institutions and jurisdictions, including FATF blacklisted countries. The transfer of monies through different jurisdictions causes one of the principal problems of tracing the asset trail. Different legislative laws and procedures prevent quick and effective investigation. This only aids the criminal/terrorist enterprise rather than law enforcement.

- **Fraud including credit card fraud**

Stockpiling of cheque-books for later misuse is a new variation on the theme of fraudulent misuse of accounts and credit cards.

- **Misuse of non-profit organisations and charities fraud**

Non-profit organisations (NPOs) are established in a wide variety of legal forms and are subject to varying degrees of control by the jurisdictions in which they are located. Given their diversity, the FATF has adopted a definition of NPOs which is based on their function rather than on their legal form, i.e. 'any legal entity that engages in the raising or disbursing of funds for charitable, religious, cultural, educational, social, fraternal or humanitarian purposes, or for the purposes of carrying out some other types of good works'.

The potential misuse of NPOs by terrorist groups can take many forms. One possibility is the establishment of an NPO with a stated charitable purpose, but which actually exists only to channel funds to a terrorist organisation. Another possibility is that an NPO with a humanitarian or charitable purpose is infiltrated by the terrorists and their supporters, often without the knowledge of the donors or the members of staff or management. Still another possibility is for the organisation to serve as the intermediary or cover for the movement of funds, usually on an international basis. In some cases, the NPO support function could extend to the movement and logistical support of the terrorists themselves.

Reporting suggests that not all charitable or goodwill institutions are regulated to this extent. In particular, charities do not always publish full accounts of the projects which their fundraising has helped to finance.

There are known cases of charities being used to raise funds for terrorist purposes. One investigation arose as a consequence of a suspicious transaction report. A bank disclosed that an individual who allegedly was earning a salary of £12,000 per annum had a turnover in the account of £250,000. A financial investigation revealed that the individual did not exist and that the account, fraudulently obtained, was linked to a Middle East charity. A fraud was being perpetrated for the purpose of raising funds for a terrorist organisation. Donations were paid into an account and the additional charitable payment was being claimed back from the government. The donation was then returned to the donor. This fraud resulted in over £800,000 being fraudulently obtained.

- *Drug trafficking*

Drugs can be a highly profitable source of funds and are used by some groups to finance other activities. Many terrorist groups are not directly involved in the importation or distribution of the drugs but exact a levy for the drug suppliers to operate within a certain area or community.

Such extortion, often known as protection money, is far less risky than being responsible for organising the supply and distribution of the drugs. The supply of controlled narcotic substances is a high priority for virtually all law enforcement agencies throughout the world and large resources are dedicated to investigation.

## Laundering through the financial system

While terrorist groups may support themselves with funding from illicit sources and legitimate sources, there appears to be little difference in the methods used by terrorist groups or criminal organisations to launder their funds, i.e. to hide or obscure the link between the source of the funds and their eventual destinations or purpose.

Bank accounts have been used in the following ways to launder terrorist funds.

- **Legitimate accounts**

It has been observed that individuals may run a number of accounts with several banks. It is not unusual for the accounts with one bank to be used for domestic purposes, while accounts based at another are for 'business purposes'. Into the former a salary or benefits may be paid, while the latter will benefit from money transfers and cheque payments. Substantial value to the investigation can be obtained from the audit trail associated with those money movements, particularly when linked to additional intelligence.

- **Dormant accounts**

On occasions, dormant accounts are used by terrorists to establish a legend upon which additional frauds are perpetrated. Facilities can be accessed which include the obtaining of bank loans, the payments of which will invariably not be met.

Dormant accounts are also used to receive monies from support members abroad. Once again, the terrorist uses a number of banks, holding an account in each of them. Two of the accounts might contain a minimal sum, believed to be for two purposes: (a) in order to keep it open; and (b) to ensure that undue attention is not drawn to it. At a strategic time, a transfer is received into the account to enable the purchase of terrorist material. The sum is eroded by the daily removal of the maximum cash amount from automatic teller machines. This continues until the entire transfer sum has been removed, which might take several months. The location of such withdrawals can prove to be of great assistance to the investigation.

- **Telegraphic transfers**

This can be effected by the use of banks or wire companies. Certain wire transfer companies appear to be used in preference to others. Enquiries to date suggest that those based in retail outlets containing video cameras are used to a much lesser extent than those where the wire transfer is franchised to a small, more localised unit. However, the use of these facilities is also determined by the ease of both sending and receiving the money. Indeed, certain companies do not even request documentation, requiring only the use of a pre-agreed question and answer prior to release of the transferred sum.

- **Money service businesses and alternative remittance systems**

Given that many sources of terrorist funding (extortion and drug trafficking, for example) generate a high volume of cash, terrorists often channel funds through bureaux, money changers and other dealers in foreign currency to finance their operations abroad. Money may pass through several jurisdictions before reaching its final destination. UK firms that carry out such business under FSA or Customs supervision should be aware of the risks in this area. Use of the informal money or transfer value system e.g. *hawala, hundi, fei-chien* and the black market *peso* exchange have also been detected in relation to terrorist financing activity.

# 9. Correspondent Banking

By their nature, correspondent banking relationships create a situation in which a credit institution carries out financial transactions on behalf of customers from another institution. This indirect relationship means that the correspondent bank provides services for individuals or entities for which it has neither verified the identities nor obtained first-hand knowledge of the respondent's customers. In correspondent banking therefore, the correspondent institution must rely on the respondent bank having performed all the necessary due diligence and continuous monitoring of its own customers' account activity.

An additional risk incurred by the correspondent bank is that a foreign respondent bank may apply less stringent anti-money laundering standards due to weaker laws and regulations, inadequate regulatory supervision or failures in applying standards or internal controls. While the correspondent bank may be able to determine the legislation in effect for the respondent bank, it is much more difficult to know the degree and effectiveness of the supervisory regime to which the respondent is subject.

A further risk is the existence of sub-respondents through which a respondent bank may itself be offering correspondent banking facilities to other credit institutions. One FATF member stated that some banks offering correspondent facilities may not be asking their respondents about the extent to which the latter offers such facilities to other institutions. This oversight has meant in certain cases that the correspondent bank is even further removed from knowing the identities or business activities of these sub-respondents, or even the types of financial services they provide.

There are also increased difficulties in monitoring the individual transactions involved in large volume correspondent accounts since the bank is usually not in contact with the originator or the beneficiary of such transactions.

# 10. Corruption, PEPs and Private Banking

Examples of senior government officials involved in corruption and other types of proceeds generating crime are no longer rare occurrences. In the past few years several high-visibility corruption cases involving 'politically exposed persons' and the laundering of vast amounts of criminal proceeds through various FATF jurisdictions have been detected and investigated.

A criminal or PEP will generally seek out private banking services, as they offer the ideal opportunity for them, their family members and close associates to carry out sophisticated and/or complex financial transactions that will further protect their illicit assets. Since a private bank is often involved in helping the client to invest or protect his or her assets, a private bank that fails to apply due diligence could find itself unwittingly assisting a corrupt politician to set up nominees and shell companies, ensuring that the beneficial ownership remains hidden.

## Appendix B

# Examples of Potentially Suspicious Activity and Transactions

Financial Sector businesses, professional firms and other relevant businesses may wish to make additional enquiries in the following circumstances:

## Banking Transactions

### Cash Transactions

- Unusually large cash deposits made by an individual or company whose ostensible business activities would normally be generated by cheques and other instruments.

- Substantial increases in cash deposits of any individual or business without apparent cause, especially if such deposits are subsequently transferred within a short period out of the account and/or to a destination not normally associated with the customer.

- Customers who deposit cash by means of numerous credit slips so that the total of each deposit is unremarkable, but the total of all the credits is significant.

- Company accounts whose transactions, both deposits and withdrawals, are denominated by cash rather than the forms of debit and credit normally associated with commercial operations (for example cheques, letters of credit or bills of exchange).

- Customers who constantly pay in or deposit cash to cover requests for bankers drafts, money transfers or other negotiable and readily marketable money instruments.

- Customers who seek to exchange large quantities of low denomination notes for those of higher denomination.

- Frequent exchange of cash into other currencies.

- Branches that have a great deal more cash transactions than usual. (Head office statistics detect aberrations in cash transactions.)

- Customers whose deposits contain counterfeit notes or forged instruments.

- Customers transferring large sums of money to or from overseas locations with instructions for payment in cash.

- Large cash deposits using night safe facilities, thereby avoiding direct contact with bank or building society staff.

## Accounts

- Customers who wish to maintain a number of trustee or client accounts which do not appear consistent with the type of business, including transactions which involve nominee names.

- Customers who have numerous accounts and pay in amounts of cash to each of them in circumstances in which the total of credits would be a large amount.

- Any individual or company whose account shows virtually no normal personal banking or business related activities, but is used to receive or disburse large sums which have no obvious purpose or relationship to the account holder and/or his business (for example a substantial increase in turnover on an account).

- Reluctance to provide normal information when opening an account, providing minimal or fictitious information or, when applying to open an account, providing information that is difficult or expensive for the financial institution to verify.

- Customers who appear to have accounts with several financial institutions within the same locality, especially when the bank or building society is aware of a regular consolidation process from such accounts prior to a request for onward transmission of the funds.

- Matching of payments out with credits paid in by cash on the same or previous day.

- Paying in large third party cheques endorsed in favour of the customer.

- Large cash withdrawals from a previously dormant/inactive account, or from an account which has just received an unexpected large credit from abroad.

- Customers who together, and simultaneously, use separate tellers to conduct large cash transactions or foreign exchange transactions.

- Greater use of safe deposit facilities; increased activity by individuals; the use of sealed packets deposited and withdrawn.

- Companies' representatives avoiding contact with the branch.

- Substantial increases in deposits of cash or negotiable instruments by a professional firm or company, using client accounts or in-house company or trust accounts, especially if the deposits are promptly transferred between other client company and trust accounts.

- Customers who show an apparent disregard for accounts offering more favourable terms.

- Customers who decline to provide information that in normal circumstances would make the customer eligible for credit or for other banking services that would be regarded as valuable.

- Insufficient use of normal banking facilities, for example avoidance of high interest rate facilities for large balances.

- Large number of individuals making payments into the same account without an adequate explanation.

## International Banking/Trade Finance

- Customer introduced by an overseas branch, affiliate or other bank based in countries where production of drugs or drug trafficking may be prevalent.

- Use of letters of credit and other methods of trade finance to move money between countries where such trade is not consistent with the customer's usual business.

- Customers who make regular and large payments, including wire transactions, that cannot be clearly identified as *bona fide* transactions to, or receive regular and large payments from, countries which are commonly associated with the production, processing or marketing of drugs, proscribed terrorist organisations or which are tax havens.

- Building up of large balances, not consistent with the known turnover of the customer's business, and subsequent transfer to account(s) held overseas.

- Unexplained electronic fund transfers by customers on an in and out basis or without passing through an account.

- Frequent requests for the issuing of travellers' cheques, foreign currency drafts or other negotiable instruments.

- Frequent paying in of travellers' cheques or foreign currency drafts, particularly if they originate from overseas.

- Customers who show apparent disregard for arrangements offering more favourable terms.

## Institution Employees and Agents

- Changes in employee characteristics, for example lavish life styles or avoiding taking holidays.

- Changes in employee or agent performance, for example the salesman selling products for cash has a remarkable or unexpected increase in performance.

- Any dealing with an agent where the identity of the ultimate beneficiary or counterpart is undisclosed, contrary to normal procedure for the type of business concerned.

## Secured and Unsecured Lending

- Customers who repay problem loans unexpectedly.

- Request to borrow against assets held by the financial institution or a third party, where the origin of the assets is not known or the assets are inconsistent with the customer's standing.

- Request by a customer for a financial institution to provide or arrange finance where the source of the customer's financial contribution to a deal is unclear, particularly where property is involved.

- Customers who unexpectedly repay in part or full a mortgage or other loan in a way inconsistent with their earnings capacity or asset base.

## Securities and Investment Business

### New Business

- A personal client for whom verification of identity proves unusually difficult and who is reluctant to provide details.

- A corporate/trust client where there are difficulties and delays in obtaining copies of the accounts or other documents of incorporation.

- A client with no discernible reason for using the firm's service, for example clients with distant addresses who could find the same service nearer their home base, or clients whose requirements are not in the normal pattern of the firm's business and could be more easily serviced elsewhere.

- An investor introduced by an overseas bank, affiliate or other investor, when both investor and introducer are based in countries where production of drugs or drug trafficking may be prevalent.

- Any transaction in which the counterparty to the transaction is unknown.

## Dealing Patterns and Abnormal Transactions

### Dealing Patterns

- A large number of security transactions across a number of jurisdictions.

- Transactions not in keeping with the investor's normal activity, the financial markets in which the investor is active and the business which the investor operates.

- Buying and selling of a security with no discernible purpose or in circumstances which appear unusual, for example churning at the client's request.

- Low-grade securities purchased in an overseas jurisdiction, sold in Britain, with the proceeds used to purchase high grade securities.
- Bearer securities held outside a recognised custodial system.

**Abnormal Transactions**

- A number of transactions by the same counterparty in small amounts of the same security, each purchased for cash and then sold in one transaction, the proceeds being credited to an account different from the original account.
- Any transaction in which the nature, size or frequency appears unusual, for example early termination of packaged products at a loss due to front end loading, or early cancellation, especially where cash had been tendered and/or the refund cheque is to a third party.
- Transactions not in keeping with normal practice in the market to which they relate, for example with reference to market size and frequency, or at off-market prices.
- Other transactions linked to the transaction in question which could be designed to disguise money and divert it into other forms or to other destinations or beneficiaries.

## Settlements

### Payment

- A number of transactions by the same counterparty in small amounts of the same security, each purchased for cash and then sold in one transaction.
- Large transaction settlement by cash.
- Payment by way of third party cheque or money transfer where there is a variation between the account holder, the signatory and the prospective investor, must give rise to additional enquiries.

### Delivery

- Settlement to be made by way of bearer securities from outside a recognised clearing system.
- Allotment letters for new issues in the name of persons other than the client.

### Disposition

- Payment to a third party without any apparent connection with the investor.
- Settlement either by registration or delivery of securities to be made to an unverified third party.
- Abnormal settlement instructions including payment to apparently unconnected parties.

# Insurance Business

## Brokerage and Sales

New Business

- A personal lines customer for whom verification of identity proves unusually difficult, who is evasive or reluctant to provide full details.

- A corporate/trust client where there are difficulties and delays in obtaining copies of the accounts or other documents of incorporation.

- A client with no discernible reason for using the firm's service, for example clients with distant addresses who could find the same service nearer their home base, or clients whose requirements are not in the normal pattern of or inconsistent with the firm's business and could be more easily serviced elsewhere.

- An investor introduced by an overseas broker, affiliate or other intermediary, when both investor and introducer are based in countries where production of drugs or drug trafficking may be prevalent.

- Any transaction in which the insured is unknown (for example treaty reinsurance or business introduced under binding authorities).

### Abnormal Transactions

- Proposals from an intermediary not in keeping with the normal business introduced.

- Proposals not in keeping with an insured's normal requirements, the markets in which the insured or intermediary is active and the business which the insured operates.

- Early cancellation of policies with return of premium, with no discernible purpose or in circumstances which appear unusual.

- A number of policies entered into by the same insurer/intermediary for small amounts and then cancelled at the same time, the return of premium being credited to an account different from the original account.

- Any transaction in which the nature, size or frequency appears unusual, for example early termination or cancellation, especially where cash had been tendered and/or the refund cheque is to a third party.

- Assignment of policies to apparently unrelated third parties.

- Transactions not in keeping with normal practice in the market to which they relate, for example with reference to size or class of business.

- Other transactions linked to the transaction in question which could be designed to disguise money and divert it into other forms or other destinations or beneficiaries.

- Willingness to pay premium on high risks which have a likelihood of regular claims being made.

## Settlements

### Payment

- A number of policies taken out by the same insured for low premiums, each purchased for cash and then cancelled with return of premium to the third party.

- Large or unusual payment of premiums or transaction settlement by cash.

- Overpayment of premium with a request to refund the excess to a third party or different country.

- Payment by way of third party cheque or money transfer where there is a variation between the account holder, the signatory and the prospective insured.

### Disposition

- Payment of claims to a third party without any apparent connection with the investor.

- Abnormal settlement instructions, including payment to apparently unconnected parties or to countries in which the insured is not known to operate.

### Claims and Reinsurances

- Strong likelihood of risks occurring, resulting in substantial claims, with consequently high premium.

- Claims paid to persons other than the insured.

- Claims which, while appearing legitimate, occur with abnormal regularity.

- Regular small claims within premium limit.

- Treaty reinsurances with high incidence of small claims.

- Regular reinsurance claims paid overseas to third parties.

- Recent change of ownership/assignment of policies just prior to a loss.

- Abnormal loss ratios for the nature and class of risk bound under a binding authority.

## Legal Profession

Anything that is unusual or unpredictable or otherwise gives cause for suspicion or concern should lead more questions about the source of funds. It is important to remember that proceeds of crime can also arrive through the banking system.

### Unusual Settlement Requests

- Request for settlement in cash.

- Surprise payments by way of a third party cheque.

- Money transfers where there is a variation between the account holder or the signatory.

- Requests to make regular payments out of a client account.

- Settlements which are reached too easily.

### Unusual Instructions

- Why has the client chosen your firm? Could the client find the same service nearer their home?

- Are you being asked to do something that does not fit with the normal pattern of your business?

- Have instructions changed without a reasonable explanation?

- Has the transaction or activity taken an unusual turn.

### Use of a Lawyers' Client Account

- Using a lawyers' client account to transmit money in useful to criminals and money launderers – it provides anonymity and enables the funds to be commingled.

- Are you being asked to provide a banking facility when you are not undertaking any related legal work?

- Are funds received into your client account when the instructions are then cancelled and you are asked to return the money either to your client or to a third party?

- Are the funds from a foreign client being routed into and out of your country without a logical explanation?

### Loss Making Transactions

- Is the instruction likely to lead to some financial loss to your client or a third party without a logical explanation, particularly where the client appears to be unconcerned?

- Is the movement of funds between difference accounts, institutions or jurisdictions merely providing confusion with no apparent reason for the movement?

## Accountancy

**The following situations will increase the risk of money laundering and should be examined further.**

- Does the client want to use the firm's client account as a bank account?
- Is it a cash-based business where the turnover cannot be justified?
- Is there a lack of independent audit evidence?
- Is there a complex group structure with no apparent reason?
- Has there been a recent change in business activity?
- Is there evidence of intra-group trading?
- Has there been a dramatic increase in turnover?
- Does the client have high turnovers/volume from small business locations?
- Were there any transactions in the year without an immediate or obvious purpose?
- Does the client require a client account denominated in a foreign currency?
- Does the client have a history of persistent and unlikely 'errors' in tax returns.
- Is there sufficient evidence of trading activity?
- Is the client merely seeking a respectable business address to create a good impression?

## Appendix C

# FATF Guidelines: Providing Feedback to Reporting Institutions and Other Persons

## Best Practice Guidelines

### Introduction

1. The importance of providing appropriate and timely feedback to financial and other institutions which report suspicious transactions has been stressed by industry representatives and recognised by the Financial Intelligence Units which receive such reports. Indeed, such information is valuable not just to those institutions, but also to other associations, to law enforcement and financial regulators and to other government bodies. However, the provision of general and specific feedback has both practical and legal implications which need to be taken into account.

2. It is recognised that ongoing law enforcement investigations should not be put at risk by disclosing inappropriate feedback information. Another important consideration is that some countries have strict secrecy laws which prevent their financial intelligence unit from disclosing any significant amount of feedback which can be given. However, those agencies which receive suspicious transaction reports should endeavour to design feedback mechanisms and procedures which are appropriate to their laws and administrative systems, which take into account such practical and legal limitations, and yet seek to provide an appropriate level of feedback. The limitations should not be used as an excuse to avoid providing feedback, though they may provide good reasons for using these guidelines in a flexible way so as to provide adequate levels of feedback for reporting institutions.

3. Based on the types and methods of feedback currently provided in a range of FATF member countries, this set of best practice guidelines will consider why providing feedback is necessary and important. The guidelines illustrate what is best practice in providing general feedback on money laundering and the results of suspicious transaction reports by setting out the different types of feedback and other information which could be provided and the methods for providing such feedback. The guidelines also address the issue of specific or case-by-case feedback and the conflicting considerations which affect the level of specific feedback which is provided in each country. The suggestions contained herein are not mandatory requirements, but are meant to provide assistance and guidance to financial intelligence units, law enforcement and other government bodies which are involved in the receipt, analysis and investigation of suspicious transaction reports, and in the provision of feedback on those reports.

## Why is Feedback on Suspicious Transaction Reports Needed?

4. The reporting of suspicious transactions[13] by banks, non-bank financial institutions and, in some countries, other entities or persons is now regarded as an essential element of the anti-money laundering programme for every country. Recommendation 15 of the FATF 40 Recommendations states that:

   *If financial institutions suspect that funds stem from a criminal activity, they should be required to report promptly their suspicions to the competent authorities.*

5. Almost all FATF members have now implemented a mandatory system of reporting suspicious transactions, though the precise extent and form of the obligation varies from country to country. The requirement under Recommendation 15 is also supplemented by several other recommendations such as that financial institutions and their staff should receive protection from criminal or civil liability for reports made in good faith (Recommendation 16); customers must not be tipped off about reports (Recommendation 17); and financial institutions should comply with instructions from the competent authorities in relation to reports (Recommendation 18).

6. It is recognised that measures to counter money laundering will be more effective if government ministries and agencies work in partnership with the financial sector. In relation to the reporting of suspicious transactions, an important element of this partnership approach is the need to provide feedback to institutions or persons which report suspicious transactions. Financial regulators will also benefit from receiving certain feedback. There are compelling reasons why feedback should be provided:

- It enables reporting institutions to better educate their staff as to the transactions which are suspicious and which should be reported. This leads staff to make higher quality reports which are more likely to correctly identity transactions connected with criminal activity;

- It provides compliance officers of reporting institutions with important information and results, allowing them to better perform that part of their function which requires them to filter out reports made by staff which are not truly suspicious. The correct identification of transactions connected with money laundering or other types of crime allows a more efficient use of the resources of both the financial intelligence unit and the reporting institution;

- It also allows the institution to take appropriate action, for example to close the customer's account if he is convicted of an offence, or to clear his name if an investigation shows that there is nothing suspicious;

- It can lead to improved reporting and investigative procedures, and is often of benefit to the supervisory authorities which regulate the reporting institutions; and

- Feedback is one of the ways in which government and law enforcement can contribute to the partnership with the financial sector, and it provides information which demonstrates to the financial sector that the resources and effort committed by them to reporting suspicious transactions are worthwhile and that results are obtained.

7. In many countries the obligation to report suspicious transactions only applies to financial institutions. Moreover, the experience in FATF in which an obligation to report also applies to non-financial businesses or to all persons is that the vast majority of suspicious transactions reports are made by financial institutions, and in particular by banks. In recent years, though, money laundering trends suggest that money launderers have moved away from strongly regulated institutions with higher levels of internal controls, such as banks, towards less strongly regulated sectors, such as the non-bank financial institution sector and non-financial businesses. In order to promote increased awareness and co-operation in these latter sectors, FIUs need to analyse trends and provide feedback on current trends and techniques to such institutions and businesses if a comprehensive anti-money laundering strategy is to be put in place. The empirical evidence suggests that where there is increased feedback to, and co-operation with, these other sectors, this leads to significantly increased numbers of suspicious transaction reports.

## General Feedback

### *Types of Feedback*

8 Several forms of general feedback are currently provided, at both national and international levels. The type of feedback and the way in which it is provided in each country may vary because of such matters as obligations of secrecy or the number of reports being received by the FIU, but the following types of feedback are used in several countries:

(a) statistics on the number of disclosures, with appropriate breakdowns, and on the results of the disclosures;

(b) information on current techniques, methods and trends (sometimes called 'typologies'); and

(c) sanitised examples of actual money laundering cases.

9. The underlying information on which general feedback can be based is either statistics relating to the number of suspicious transaction reports and the results achieved from those reports, or cases or investigations involving money laundering (whether or not the defendant is prosecuted for a money laundering offence or for the predi-

cate offences). As these cases or investigations could result from a suspicious transaction report or from other sources of information, it is important that those agencies which provide feedback ensure that all relevant examples are included in the feedback they provide. It is also important that all relevant authorities, together with the reporting institutions, agree on the contents and form of sanitised cases, so as to prevent any subsequent difficulties for any institution or agency. It would also be beneficial if certain types of feedback, such as sanitised cases, are widely distributed, so that the benefits of this feedback are not restricted to the reporting institutions in that particular country.

## Statistics – What Types of Statistics Should Be Made available ?

10. Statistical information can be broken down into at least two categories:

   (a) that which relates to the reports received and the breakdowns that can be made of this information; and

   (b) that which relates to reports which lead to or assist in investigations, prosecutions or confiscation action. Examples of the types of statistics which could be retained are:

   • **Category (a):** Detailed information on matters such as the number of suspicious transaction reports, the number of reports by sector or institution, the monetary value of such reports and files, and the geographical areas from which cases have been referred. Information could also be retained to give a breakdown of the types of institutions which reported and the types of transactions involved in the transactions reported.

   • **Category (b):** Information on the investigation case files opened, the number of cases closed and cases referred to the prosecution authorities. Breakdowns could also be given of the year in which the report was made, the types of crimes involved and the amount of money, as well as the nationality of the parties involved and which of the three stages of a money laundering operation (placement, layering or integration) the case related to. Where appropriate, statistics could also be kept on the reports which have a direct and positive intelligence value, and an indication given of the value of those reports. This is because reports which do not lead directly to a money laundering prosecution can still provide valuable information which may lead to prosecutions or confiscation proceedings at a later date (see paragraph 18).

11. A cross-referencing of the different breakdowns of category (a) information with the types of results achieved under category (b) should enable FIUs and reporting institutions to identify those areas where reporting institutions are successfully identifying money laundering and other criminal activity. It would also identify, for example,

those areas where institutions are not reporting or are reporting suspicions which lead to below average results. As such it would be a valuable tool for all concerned. However, as with any statistics, care needs to be taken in their interpretation and in the weight that is accorded to each statistic. In order to extract the desired statistics efficiently, it is of course necessary that the suspicious transaction report form, whether it is sent on paper or online, is designed to allow the appropriate breakdowns to be made. Given the difficulties that many countries have in gathering and analysing statistics, it is essential that the amount of human resources required for this task are minimised, and that maximum use is made of technology, even if this initially requires capital expenditure or other resource inputs.

## How Often Should Statistics Be Published?

12 Statistics are the most commonly provided form of feedback and are usually included in annual reports or regular newsletters, such as those published by FIUs. Having regard to the resource implications of collecting and providing statistics, and to the other types of feedback available, the publication of an annual set of comprehensive statistics should provide adequate feedback in most countries.

13. **It is recommended that:**

- **Statistics are kept on the suspicious transaction reports received and on the results obtained from those reports, and that appropriate breakdowns are made of the available information;**

- **The statistics on the reports received are cross-referenced with the results so as to identify areas where money laundering and other criminal activity is being successfully detected;**

- **Technological resources are used to their maximum potential; and**

- **Comprehensive statistics are published at least once a year.**

## Current Techniques, Methods and Trends

14. The description of current money laundering techniques and methods will be largely based on the cases sent to the prosecution authorities, and the division of such cases into the three stages of money laundering can make it easier to distinguish between the different techniques used, though it must be recognised that it is often difficult to categorically state that a transaction falls into one stage or another. If new methods or techniques are identified, these should be described and identified, and reporting institutions should be advised of such methods as well as of current money laundering trends. Information on current trends will be derived from prosecutions, investigations or the statistics referred to above, and can usefully be linked with those statistics. An accurate description of current trends will allow financial institutions to focus on areas of current and future risk.

15. In addition to any reports that are prepared by national FIUs, there are a number of international organisations or groups which also prepare reports of trends and techniques, or hold an exercise to review such trends. The FATF holds an annual typologies exercise where law enforcement and regulatory experts from FATF members, as well as delegates from relevant observer organisations, review and discuss current trends and future threats in relation to money laundering. A public report is then published which reviews the conclusions of the experts and the trends and techniques in FATF members and other countries, as well as considering a special topic in more detail. This report is available from the FATF or the FATF Website (*http://www.oecd.org/fatf/*). In addition, Interpol publishes regular bulletins which contain sanitised case examples.

16. Other international groups, such as the Asia-Pacific Group on Money Laundering, the Caribbean Financial Action Task Force, and the Organisation of American States/Inter-American Drug Abuse Control Commission will also hold typologies exercises which could provide further information on the trends and techniques that are being used to launder money in the regions concerned. International trends could usefully be extracted and included in feedback supplied by national FIUs where they are particularly relevant, but in relation to more general information, reporting institutions should simply be made aware of how they can access such reports if they wish to. This will help to avoid information overload.

17. It is recommended that:

- New money laundering methods or techniques, as well as trends in existing techniques are described and identified, and that financial and other institutions are advised of these trends and techniques;

- Feedback on trends and techniques published by international bodies be extracted and included in feedback supplied by national FIUs only if it is particularly relevant, but that reporting institutions are made aware of how to access such reports.

## Sanitised Cases

18. This type of feedback is sometimes regarded by financial sector representatives as even more valuable than information on trends. Sanitised cases[14] are very helpful to compliance officers and front line staff, since they provide detailed examples of actual money laundering and the results of such cases, thus increasing the awareness of front line staff. Two examples of methods used to distribute this type of feedback are a quarterly newsletter and a database of sanitised cases. Both methods provide a set of sanitised cases which summarise the facts of the case, the enquiries made and a brief summary of the results. A short section drawing out the lessons to be learnt

from the case is also provided in the database. The length of the description of each case could vary from a paragraph outlining the case, through to a longer and more detailed summary.

19. Care and consideration needs to be taken in choosing appropriate cases and in their sanitisation in order to avoid any legal ramifications. In the countries which use such feedback, the examples used are generally cases which have been completed, either because the criminal proceedings are concluded or because the report was not found to be justified. Inclusion of cases where the report was unfounded can be just as helpful as those where the subject of the report was convicted on money laundering.

20. **It is recommended that sanitised cases be published or made available to reporting institutions, and that each sanitised case could include:**

- **a description of the facts;**

- **a brief summary of the results of the case;**

- **where appropriate, a description of the enquiries made by the FIU; and**

- **a description of the lessons to be learnt from the reporting and investigative procedures that were adopted in the case. Such lessons can be helpful not only to financial institutions and their staff, but also to law enforcement investigators.**

## *Other Information Which Could Be Provided*

21. In addition to general feedback of the types referred to above, there are other types of information which can be distributed to financial and other institutions using the same methods. Often this information is provided in guidance notes or annual reports, but it provides essential background information for the staff of reporting institutions and also keeps them up to date on current issues. Examples of such other information include:

- **An explanation of why money laundering takes place, a description of the money laundering process and the three stages of money laundering, including practical examples;**

- **An explanation of the legal obligation to report, to whom it applies and the sanctions (if any) for failing to report;**

- **The procedures and processes by which reports are made, analysed and investigated, and by which feedback is provided,** allow FIUs to provide information on matters such as the length of time it can take for a criminal proceeding to be finalised or to explain that even though not every report results in a prosecution for money laundering, the report could be used as evidence or intelligence which contributes to a prosecution for a criminal offence, or provides other valuable intelligence information;

- **a summary of any legislative changes** which may have been recently made in relation to the reporting regime or money laundering offences;

- **a description of current and/or future challenges for the FIU.**

### Feedback Methods

22. **Written Feedback:** As noted above, two of the most popular methods of providing general feedback are through annual reports and regular newsletters or circulars. As noted above, annual reports could usefully contain sets of statistics and description of money laundering trends. A short (for example, four-page) newsletter or circular which is published on a regular basis two or four times a year provides continuity of contact with reporting institutions. It could contain sanitised cases, legislative updates or information on current issues or money laundering methods.

23. **Meetings:** There are a range of other ways in which feedback is provided to the bodies or persons who report. Most FIUs provide such feedback through face-to-face meetings with financial institutions, wither for a specific institution or its staff, or for a broader range of institutions. Seminars, conferences and workshops are commonly used to provide training for financial institutions and their staff, and this provides a forum in which feedback is provided as part of the training and education process. Several countries have also established working or liaison groups combining the FIUs which receive the reports and representatives of the financial sector. These groups can also include the financial regulator or representatives of law enforcement agencies, and provide a regular channel of communication through which feedback, and other topics such as reporting procedures, can be discussed. Finally, staff of FIUs could use meetings with individual compliance officers as an opportunity to provide general feedback.

24. **Video:** Many countries and financial institutions or their associations have published an educational video as part of their overall anti-money laundering training and education process. Such a method of communication provides an opportunity for direct feedback to front line staff and could include material on sanitised cases, money laundering methods and other information.

25 **Electronic Information Systems** obtaining information from websites, other electronic databases or through electronic message systems have the advantage of speed, increased efficiency, reduced operating costs and better accessibility to relevant information. While the need for appropriate confidentiality and security must be maintained, consideration should be given to providing increasing feedback through a password protected or secure website or database, or by electronic mail.

26 When deciding on the methods of general feedback that are to be used, each country will have to take into account the views of the reporting institutions as to the degree to which reporting of suspicious or unusual transactions should be made public knowledge. For example, in some countries, the banks have no objection to sanitised cases becoming public information, in part because of the objective and transparent nature of the reporting system. However, in other countries, financial institutions would like to receive this type of feedback, but do not want it made available to the public as a whole. Such differing views mean that slightly different approaches may need to be taken in each country.

## Specific or Case-by-Case Feedback

27. Reporting institutions and their associations welcome prompt and timely information on the results of reports of suspicious transactions, not only so that they can improve the processes of their member institutions for identifying suspicious transactions, but also so that they can take appropriate action in relation to the customer. There is concern that by keeping a customer's account open, after a suspicious transaction report has been made, the institution may be increasing its vulnerability with respect to monies owned to them by the customer. However, specific feedback is much more difficult to provide than general feedback, for both legal and practical reasons.

28. One of the primary concerns is that ongoing law enforcement investigations should not be put at risk by providing specific feedback information to the reporting institution at a stage prior to the conclusion of the case. Another practical concern is the question of the resource implications and the best and most efficient method for providing such feedback, which will often depend on the amount of reports received by the FIU. Legal issues in some countries relate to strict secrecy laws which prevent the FIU from disclosing specific feedback, or concern general privacy laws which limit the feedback which can be provided. Finally, financial institutions are also concerned about the degree to which such feedback becomes public knowledge, and the need to ensure the safety of their staff and protect them from being called as witnesses who have to give evidence in court concerning the disclosure. This was dealt with in one country by a specific legislative amendment which prohibits suspicious transaction reports being put in evidence or even referred to in court.

29. Given these limitations and concern, current feedback information provided by receiving agencies to reporting institutions on specific cases is more limited than general feedback. The only information which appears to be provided in most countries is an acknowledgement of receipt of the suspicious transaction report. In some countries this is provided through an automatic, computer-generated response,

which would be the most efficient method of responding. The other form of specific feedback which is relied on in many countries is informal feedback through unofficial contacts. Often this is based on the police officer or prosecutor who is investigating the case following up the initial report, and serving the reporting institution with a search warrant or some other form of compulsory court order requiring further information to be produced. Although this gives the institution some further feedback information, it will only be interim information which does not show the result of the case, and the institution is left uncertain as to when it will receive the information.

30. Depending on the degree to which the practical and legal considerations referred to in Paragraph 28 apply in each country, other types of specific feedback are provided; this includes regular advice on cases that are closed, information on whether a case has been passed on for investigation and the name of the investigating police officer or district, and advice on the result of a case when it is concluded. In most countries, feedback is not normally provided during the pendancy of any investigation involving the report.

31. Having regard to current practice and the concerns identified above, and taking into account the requirements imposed by any national secrecy or privacy legislation, and subject to other limitations such as risk to the investigation and resource implications, it is recommended that whenever possible, the following -specific feedback is provided (and that time limits could also be determined by appropriate authorities so that it is assured that the feedback is timely), namely that:

(a) Receipt of the report should be acknowledged by the FIU;

(b) If the report will be subject to a fuller investigation, the institution could be advised of the agency that will investigate the report, if the agency does not believe this would adversely affect the investigation; and

(c) If a case is closed or completed, whether because of a concluded prosecution, because the report was found to relate to a legitimate transaction or for other reasons, then the institution should receive information on that decision or result.

## Conclusion

32. In relation to both specific and general feedback, it is necessary that an efficient system exists for determining whether the report led or contributed to a positive result, whether by way of prosecution or confiscation, or through its intelligence value. Whatever the administrative structure of the government agencies involved in collecting intelligence or investigating and prosecuting criminality, it is essential

that whichever agency is responsible for providing feedback receives the information and results upon which that feedback is based. If the FIU which receives the report is the body responsible, this will usually require the investigating officers or the prosecutor to provide the FIU with feedback on the results in a timely and efficient way. One method of efficiently achieving this could be through the use of a standard reporting form, combined with a set distribution list. Failure to provide such information will make the feedback received by reporting institutions far less accurate or valuable.

33. It is clear that there is considerable diversity in the volume, types and methods of general and specific feedback currently being provided. The types and methods of feedback are undoubtedly improving, and many countries are working closely with their financial sectors to try to increase the amount of feedback and reduce any limitations, but it is clear that the provision of feedback is still at an early stage of development in most countries. Further co-operative exchange of information and ideas is thus necessary for the partnership between FIUs, law enforcement and the financial sector to work more effectively, and for countries to provide not only an increased level of feedback, but also where feasible, greater uniformity.

# Notes

1  Higgins, J. Kevin (2000). 'Offshore Financial Services: An Introduction', *The Eastern Caribbean Banker*, Vol. 2.
2  Response of the Working Group on Offshore Centres, 'Financial Stability Forum', April 2000.
3  Source: UK Electronic Money Association on mitigating the risks of money laundering and compliance with the identification requirements.
4  'Clean Money, Dirty Money, Corruption and Money Laundering in the UK,' Transparency International (UK), Policy Research Paper 002, June 2003.
5  This also captures private banking.
6  This includes, inter alia, consumer credit, mortgage credit, factoring, with or without recourse and finance of commercial transactions (including forfeiting).
7  This does not extend to financial leasing arrangements in relation to consumer products.
8  This applies to financial activity in both the formal or informal sector, e.g. alternative remittance activity. See the Interpretative Note to FATF Special Recommendation VI. It does not apply to any natural or legal person that provides financial institutions solely with message or other support systems for transmitting funds. See the Interpretative Note to Special Recommendation VII.
9  This applies both to insurance undertakings and to insurance intermediaries (agents and brokers).
10 References to financial institutions in the FATF recommendations also relate to the designated professions and businesses.
11 Recommendation 12 extends the customer due diligence procedures for financial institutions that are contained in FATF Recommendations 5 and 6 to the professions and designated businesses.
12 Recommendation 12 extends the record-keeping procedures for financial institutions that are contained in FATF Recommendation 10 to the professions and designated businesses.
13 In some jurisdictions the obligation is to report unusual transactions, and these guidelines should be read so as to include unusual transactions within any references to suspicious transactions, where appropriate.
14 Sanitised cases are cases which have had all specific identifying features removed.